Deliverability Inferno

Helping Email Marketers Understand the Journey from Purgatory to Paradise

Chris Arrendale

Atlanta Georgia

"Too often, deliverability is approached like the dark arts of email marketing—only to be accessed by a select few. Chris blows the doors off the gates of email marketing hell with his pragmatic approach, expertise, and wit."

—Morgan Stewart, CEO, Trendline Interactive

"Email is supposed to be dead, per social media nuts, but my feedback, edits, and additions to this paper were written on 100% recycled spam!"

—Dennis Dayman, Chief Privacy and Security Officer, Return Path

"Chris is one of the foremost experts in the world on email deliverability. His book is a must-read for anyone seeking a deeper understanding of the challenges marketers face in ensuring their messages are seen by their best customers."

—Simms Jenkins, Founder & CEO of BrightWave

and Author of *The New Inbox* and *The Truth About Email Marketing*

"*Deliverability Inferno* is a must read for any marketer who is using email as part of their multi-channel marketing mix. Arrendale does a superb job in addressing the ins-and-outs of email deliverability and taking a subject that is often complex and hard to understand and breaking it down into practical insights that will help organizations get more value from their email marketing and enable them to better reach their target buyers and customers."

—Carlos Hidalgo, CEO, VisumCx

DELIVERABILITY INFERNO

Published by The Arrendale Group
1995 North Park Place, Suite 300
Atlanta GA 30339
U.S.A.

www.deliverabilityinferno.com

ISBN: 978-0-9998801-0-4

Printed in the United States of America

Nine Challenges of Deliverability

Acknowledgements

Foreword by Jay Jhun

Introduction
Deliverability Versus Delivery

First Challenge
Content

Second Challenge
Lists

Third Challenge
Bounces

Fourth Challenge
Complaints

Fifth Challenge
Spam Traps

Sixth Challenge
Blacklists

Seventh Challenge
Authentication

Eighth Challenge
Compliance

Ninth Challenge
Technology

Companies in Paradise

References and Resources

About the Author

Acknowledgements

I want to thank the many people who are working to expand the science, art, and understanding of email deliverability. Email deliverability has been a passion of mine for many years and I am excited to have this book published. Doing great work, with a great team, for great clients is why I love coming to work every day. I have been influenced by the actions of many whose work and stories are recorded in this book. Several people directly helped me by reviewing and advising us on various iterations of this book:

∞ To Mary Arrendale - Where do I begin? You are the greatest mother in the world and have done everything for me. I try to make you proud every day and to be the best son you could ask for. Thank you for all of your help and support in life and on this book.

∞ To Meme and Papa - Since I was born, you both have been by my side. From helping raise me, going to furniture auctions, to paying for my entire education, you both have always (and will always) be with me. Thank you for pushing me to be the best in every part of my life. I am where I am in my life because of both of you.

∞ To Christy Arrendale - The best sister in the entire world. You have always pushed me to go the extra mile and thank you for being my best friend.

∞ To Lamar Arrendale - For all of your help and support in life and business. Thank you for your continued encouragement and feeling no pain along the way.

∞ To James and Jeff - For continuing to push me to be a better man and entrepreneur. Thank you both for always being there to give me support when I need it most.

∞ To Tony and Brenda Swartzlander - For the best in-laws that I could ever ask for. You both are role models and an inspiration to me. Thank you for your support on this book.

∞ To my nieces and nephews - Make sure you read the book! Love each and every one of you.

∞ To my brother and sister-in-laws - Each and every one of you has played an important role in my life and in this book.

∞ To my entire family that loves me and worries about me every day!

∞ The great people at Oxford College and Emory University family (a real family!). I am Chris Arrendale today because of my education, experiences, leadership opportunities, time management, and love from the entire University. I love each and every one of you for what you have done for my family and me.

∞ All the wonderful people at Southern Polytechnic State University and the education I received to help boost my career.

∞ To my M3AAWG family for continuing to allow me to provide leadership in the space and for ongoing training to make the community better.

∞ The DMA & EEC have been very influential to get our deliverability training and certification materials out to marketers around the world.

∞ All the great people at the International Association of Privacy Professionals (IAPP) and the training I continue to receive.

∞ My TEAM at Inbox Pros. You are the best group of people that I have ever worked with, and thank you for your help with this book.

∞ My wonderful clients and colleagues that push us to do amazing work each and every day. I couldn't have put together these pages and great stories without you!

∞ Finally, Candi Sue Cross as proofreader, editor, and advisor, who helped guide me to the final manuscript that is now this book. Thank you for the laughs and organization!

I dedicate this book to my wife, Amanda Arrendale. My business partner, CFO, best friend, wife, purdy, and the love of my life. Your help and guidance has made me the man I am today. Thank you for putting up with hectic schedules, business travel, crazy ideas, and working around the clock! We have made so many good memories and look forward to making many more together. You are my biggest cheerleader and always push me to my greatest potential. Without you, this book would not be possible. I love you.

—Chris Arrendale

November 2017

Foreword

When Chris asked me if I would write the foreword to his book, I was, of course, honored and humbled. Certainly it couldn't be any harder than writing a blog post, right? Well, I agreed but soon started thinking about what on Earth could I say that would convince you to read, ponder, consume, digest and master email deliverability. Then I discovered that Dante Alighieri's *Inferno* was part of his inspiration for talking about the craft that he loves and has proven to me and my clients over the years that he has mastered.

'So, you're saying that learning about email deliverability is like entering the nine circles of hell?'

Of course not! In fact, the nine chapters that lie ahead for you are what I wish every marketer would read to truly understand how email marketing actually works (as in, how an email gets from one deploying an email to landing on your mobile phone's email client) because it is not nearly as simple as you think it is, but it also isn't rocket science.

Equally, experienced email marketers who have earned their stripes designing, coding, deploying and reporting on email campaigns will agree that ensure, by incorporating these fundamentals about email deliverability, that when you say speak as a subject matter expert on email marketing, people listen.

I've been in the business of email marketing for over a decade now. To me, email marketing has been the gift that keeps on giving to me professionally as a digital marketer because it has always been (and will always be) the perfect blend of the left-brain (technology, data, analytics) and right-brain (creativity, brand expression) disciplines in the 21st century marketing world.

If you are a left-brain type of person, you'll really dig this book. No more fuzzy logic around how an email gets from point A to point B. No more depending on vague, generic knowledgebase articles about deliverability best practices to read through. No more fear of putting your company on a Spamhaus blacklist or placing your company's precious emails in your customers' junk folder. So, if that sounds like you and it sounds good, read on!

If you skew more right-brain, you'll walk away with enough knowledge to hang with those left-brain email kids. But more than that, you might find yourself with newer, stronger feelings about the holistic customer experience, Seth Godin's notion of permission, and what a disservice it is to be sending the same email creative to your entire database.

I applaud you for investing your time (and for Chris's sake, a couple of bucks) into learning more about email deliverability. In the heyday of email service provider conferences, the sexy sessions and topics were around creative design, subject lines, coding techniques, A/B testing and all the other usual suspects. Yet, it was always the deliverability sessions that were quietly at capacity because the savvier email marketers who'd been to all the other sessions realized that understanding email deliverability was a missing piece of the puzzle they were trying to solve. They knew that the real devil in email marketing was getting blacklisted by Spamhaus, getting bulked by Google's Postmaster or worse yet, getting sued as part of a legal action for violating CAN-SPAM or CASL.

The fact of the matter is that email marketing is a complex puzzle and the puzzle varies from company to company, without fail. It's not because how email marketing works is different for each organization. Rather, it's because stakeholders, knowledge gaps, budgetary silos, business priorities and ultimately, audiences are completely unique.

Ten years ago, I thought that perhaps it would take a decade or so for the C-Suite to finally see the value in (and hire the right people to lead) digital marketing. Digital marketing was the upstart unknown that was getting fractional attention in marketing budgets. Here we are in 2017, and while there are certainly more marketing leaders now that 'get it' when it comes to digital marketing, there are still some serious blind spots that are only now coming to light.

Strangely enough, the blind spot manifests itself in the old business adage that 'Customer is King.' Suddenly old wisdom is coming front and center again as customer experience takes center stage and marketers try to tailor and personalize the digital journey of their customer, not by segments, but at the individual level, at scale, in near real-time.

The blind spot I'm referring to is the bloodthirsty side of marketers that treat their customers as numbers, not as people. A number is a street address that you use to print a brochure about lakefront property, slap some postage on and all you have is upside if they respond. A customer is someone who has feelings about randomly receiving an email about said lakefront property liquidation, reports abuse and damages your ability to send to other customers in the future. Yeah, email marketing is personal because your customers put the *person* in personal.

Hence, we have the fanatical, unwavering, almost cavalier stance that ISP postmasters and Spamhaus take on behalf of your customers as it pertains to bad email marketing behavior. *Deliverability Inferno* is going to help you see things from their point of view and perhaps give you pause to put yourself in your customers' shoes as you peruse your own junk/spam folder and see who have been the poor, unfortunate souls to land in email purgatory.

The last thing I'll say before you get on with the actual book is that in all the time I've known and worked with Chris, I can say unequivocally that his advice has never steered me or my clients wrong. I'm so excited and proud that he's put pen to paper with these fundamentals so that not only would other marketers avoid the pitfalls of bad email marketing behavior but that more email marketers master the craft completely and that email marketing can rightly sit in a high position that we both believe it deserves.

—Jay Jhun

President, Atlanta Interactive Marketing Association

Introduction

Deliverability Versus Delivery

History of Email

Email is still the cheapest, most effective form of communication. Instagram or forever-a-gram will not replace the full circumference of messaging in email. (Okay, if your target market is people who listen to Justin Bieber, *maybe* Instagram is better since they may not be using email.) Campaign Monitor reports that the average ROI on one email is $44. It depends on what you are selling. Email is often used as a way to keep a record of a communication or to archive information. For example: if you signed up for a coupon that does not expire, it is tougher to do that in social media than email. If your friend is asking where you got that sweater, it may be easier to search for it in Gmail than in social media.

I was watching a video earlier. They mentioned that for the business-to-consumer audience, it is easier to reach people in social. For business-to-business, email is still the most significant channel because you're trying to reach your buyer in different ways. Cookies, tracking and segmentation from your website help determine what that user wants to purchase. If you are an effective marketer, you can send an email campaign with that specific product they want at the right time. And then hopefully they will convert. Everybody always thinks, *how do I get to Gmail*, whereas my take is, how can I get them to click and convert to a buyer?

Taking a walk through time with me in order to understand new complexities will help you achieve that goal faster. Many years ago, when email didn't even consist of Gmail yet, AOL and Yahoo! were the primary providers. I'm sure you remember receiving more pure spam (like Viagra ads, ugh) into your Inbox. Filters weren't efficient or effective. What has changed over the course of time is a term called *engagement.* Engagement then prompted the need for stronger *permissions* and *authentication*, along with modern resources to meet their requirements. Like the Environmental Protection Agency cleans up pollution from our natural environments, marketers should be good stewards for online space while optimizing the facets of their email program.

Always focus on the user, the recipient opening it. Are they clicking, scrolling, saving, deleting without reading it, reading it and sharing it? A recipient can take all of these actions with your one email and each of their actions signifies a different meaning. Mailbox providers are monitoring this activity and using it to determine Inbox placement these days. They take into consideration content, reputation and volume, but engagement is king. That has become the forefront over the past sixteen years.

Authentication is like a passport when you are going through airport security. There are a few forms of email authentication: SPF, DKIM. You need both. These are your passport to the network, proving you are the brand you say you are. I'm sure you get emails from lots of brands. If you look in the header, it will say SPF pass or fail or may not even say anything.

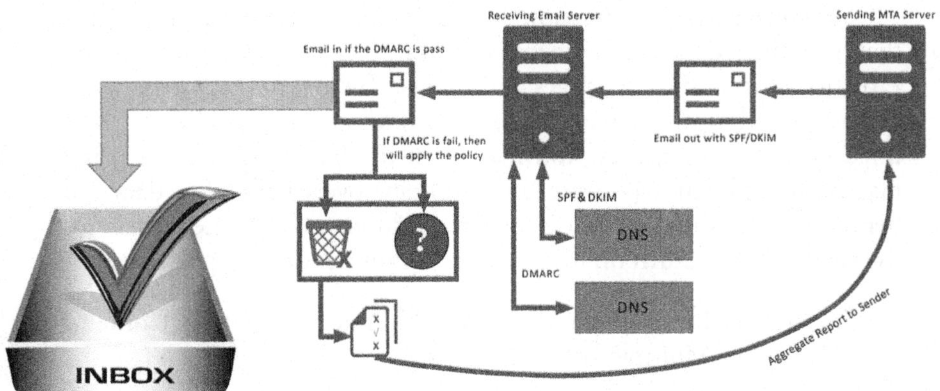

Figure 1. The Path of Email Authentication

In plain terms, authentication ensures the authenticity and protection of a brand. It attempts to protect a legitimate brand against phishing, or fraudulent emails. "Reset your password from Bank of America." Sound familiar? Phishing scams are on the rise, often disguising themselves as big banks and other financial services companies that do business with millions of customers and merchants. They want to steal private and sensitive information. All too often, it works. But over the years, these junk emails have become more malicious, targeting vulnerable retirees on fixed income, for example, and taking them for a ride—all via a clandestine email.

Permission is also very important. Over the course of time, there has been a change in the thought process of email. When you give a favorite brand your email address, whether a Nordstrom Rack or Outback, you just assume you will receive a lot of marketing emails. But permission is "the law," as we see in Canada and the EU in their electronic and digital communication laws. Canada enforces the Canadian Anti-Spam Legislation (CASL), which has explicit opt-in permission before you can send marketing communication. For May of 2018, the EU will enforce the General Data Protection Regulation (GDPR) focused on residents in all of the EU member states requiring explicit opt-in permission before you can send marketing emails.

Do you have permission to send to me? If not, I may mark your messages as spam or report you or outright ignore it. All of these receiver actions affect email deliverability. If someone is phishing your brand and domain, over time, it will degrade your brand, IP, and reputation. Email will be dumped in the junk folder and you may never know why.

So, engagement, permission and authentication are the three areas that have changed email marketing drastically. I started my agency, Inbox Pros, to address these changes for clients. *Deliverability Inferno* is an extension of this outreach to marketers. You won't learn this information in school or in an agency. You may learn the hard way, such as being blacklisted and you may never know it. Being overwhelmed by data and demands, your shiny email campaigns could be stuck at the bottom of the well with no return on investment or imminent Inbox placement.

So, back to the email world of today: Volume. Reputation. Content. Authentication. Multiple layers of filtering.

Deliverability gauntlet, deliverability inferno. This all sounds so

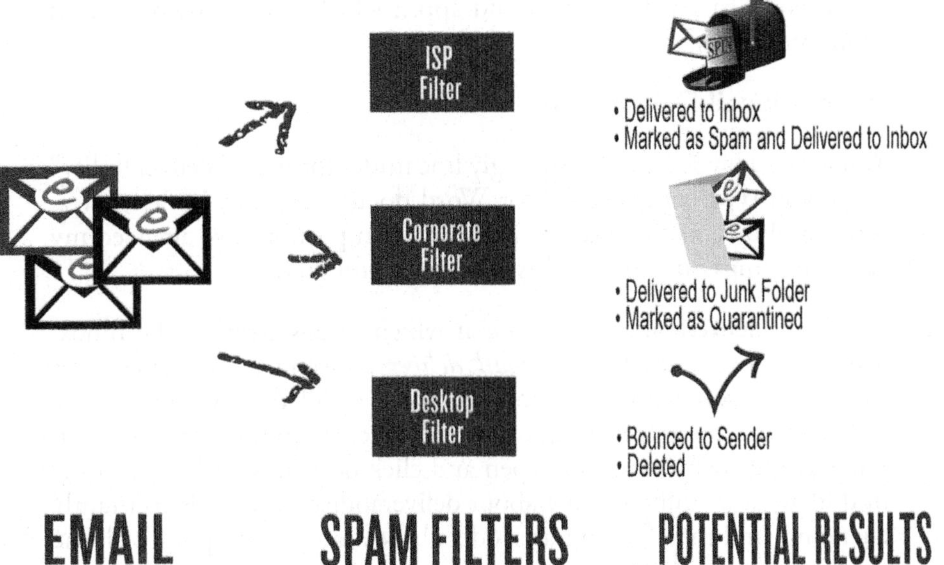

Figure 2. Email Filtering

foreboding and tedious, but right this very minute, approximately 20 million emails are being crafted. Though tied to marketing dollars and marketer jobs, many of these emails will not make it to the Inbox. They will never be seen. They will disappear in...*inferno.*

Having worked in the front, back and side houses (or halls) of the deliverability business, I can guarantee that every marketer wants higher opens, clicks and conversions.

With 3.3 billion registered accounts in operation as of 2012 (75 percent consumer; 25 percent business), email is here to stay as an essential form of global connection, communication, sales lead, and sales conversion. On the other hand, email can also light a flame under your brand's reputation, make you look obsolete against your competition, and assign an unfavorable label like "unprofessional," "amateur," "annoying" to you if your content is not relevant, frequent or infrequent (depending on the subscriber), compliant, beneficial, attention-grabbing, informational, entertaining...you're catching on.

There is so much to know and apply, which is why you've entered *Deliverability Inferno*.

What is Email Deliverability?

While you may see the red, squiggly line under the word "deliverability" when you type it in an email or Word document, it is, in fact, a real term used by email marketers, and it is so important, I've amassed my career findings on deliverability in this helpful guide.

Email deliverability is the rate at which emails arrive in the Inbox. This can be confused with *email delivery*, meaning your email was successfully sent without bouncing. Thus, email deliverability is one of the most important metrics since all other metrics depend upon it. For example, customers can't open and click on your email if they can't find it! Yet, one thing to note about deliverability is that it is constantly changing, and therefore, we as senders have a duty to keep up with the changing times. Mailbox providers are adapting to new spammer tactics and techniques to protect their networks.

At this stage in your marketing career, you're probably familiar with terms such as click-through rate, open rate, and bounce rate. Unfortunately, we often see that many small to medium companies end their email marketing analysis here. While these metrics are valuable they do not provide a complete picture of your email marketing efforts.

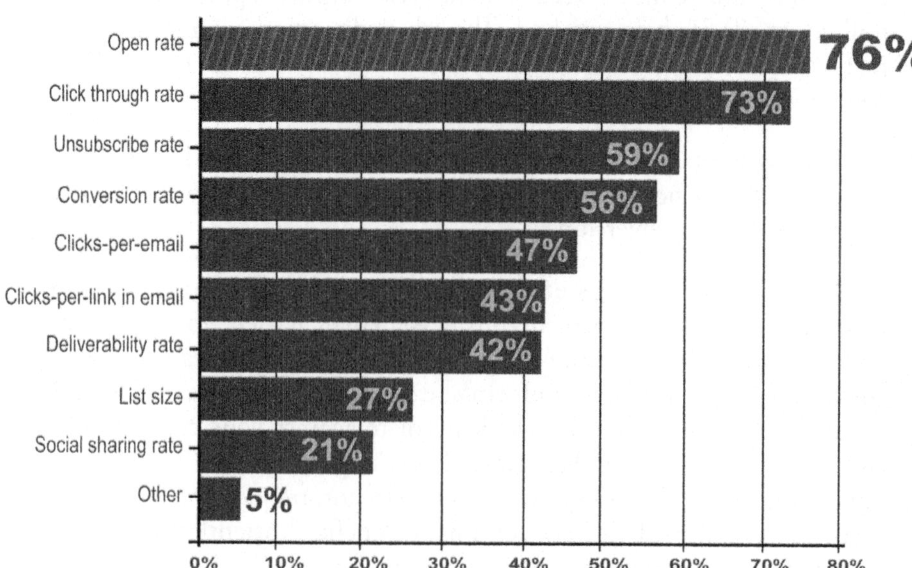

Figure 3. What Email Metrics are Tracked (Source: Progress Follow)

What if I asked you, "What is your reputation with Gmail, Yahoo!, Comcast, or Barracuda?" Would you know where to look, or what to look for? Are your emails going into the spam folder or the updates tab?

This is where we enter the realm of email deliverability, and understanding the importance of email deliverability for modern marketers.

Then you may ask, "How do I know if my emails are going into the spam folder?" You're not alone in asking this question. Opens and clicks will help you understand Inbox placement. There is not system or report that will give you Inbox placement status on every email campaign you send. As email spam filters and mailbox providers (MBPs) beef up their delivery algorithms, marketers are beginning to understand the importance of email deliverability. The days of more volume equating to more money are long gone. Quality over quantity. Let me repeat that: *Long gone!*

More email activity does not equal more profit.

Accordingly, when we speak to marketers, we find that these old email marketing metrics are so thoroughly entrenched that the real epiphany happens when they realize their click rate stinks because their deliverability stinks.

Peek at Paradise from Purgatory

Email deliverability is centered on a core philosophy of putting your recipients first. If you take this approach and embrace it over time, you will see your deliverability increase substantially.

The first steps are sending emails people want rather than emails you want, maintaining basic list practices such as confirmed opt-in, removal of unengaged users, and easy unsubscribes, and refraining from spam-like phrases, words and links to low-reputation websites. Sneaky list acquisition will not go unpunished, and in some cases is illegal, so think twice before buying that list!

While you are focusing on following all these best practices it is very important to know if you are on a shared or dedicated IP. This information is crucial in formulating your deliverability strategy, so if you're unsure, we will help get you through that challenge, too, since being on a shared IP could be killing your delivery.

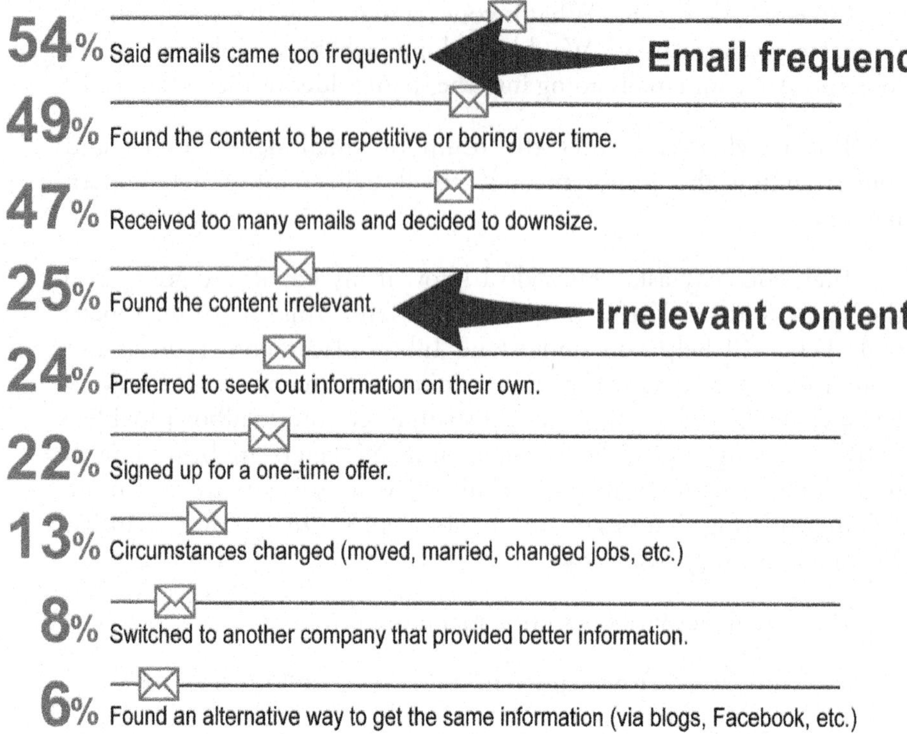

Figure 4. Reasons People Unsubscribe

Inbox Inferno (It's Not Too Late to Turn Back!)

While on a business trip to Paris, I visited the spectacular Musee du Louvre. While there, I fixated on a piece of art from Milton's "Paradise Lost." A guy looking at the stream of lava flowing in front of him and then a huge building off to the side. Immediately, I thought of a gatekeeper monitoring all moves between an email sender, or marketer, and a recipient, and understanding what that gatekeeper wants in order to grant entry to the Inbox.

This book will provide great detail of the nine challenges to overcome for making it to Inbox paradise, but if you often divide your attention throughout the day and stop to read emails like I do (I hate the number pop-up on my iPhone indicating any unread messages—call me compulsive.), it's obvious the subject line is the first thing a gatekeeper sees about your brand and subsequent message. Make it pop and stand out. I use a saying in my presentations, "tying dollars to deliverability." When senders finally get around to look at campaign

Figure 5. Scene from John Milton's 17th century epic poem, "Paradise Lost" (Source: Art Resource)

statistics, they look at opens and clicks, but they're not looking at other metrics that you can tie to dollars: conversions and complaints. Look at email deliverability as dollars. What if these people aren't seeing your message and you have 100,000 contacts in your database?

Since you're agreeing to journey through the inferno, I will uncover complexities for you to achieve higher ROI. For the squeamish and faint at heart, don't worry; you will not see darkness and horror or lurid imagery. In fact, the only horror you may experience is deliverability inertia for not doing anything with the valuable, rare information you learn.

What is your campaign worth? Everything if it reaches the Inbox!

Sixth Sense: Social

Before we get started, I will point out there is much ado about social media and the role it plays in marketing and advertising. Well, brands aren't leveraging social media correctly from email. If contacts opt-out of emails because it's not their thing, they can still follow the company on social media. No one looks at deliverability from a business perspective. From the business side, you must look at multiple data points including social media and all the tools that are available, understanding lists, understanding content, to make best decision for your business and overall practice.

If I told everybody, "use these ten best practices," few people would send that email. If I recommend double opt-in to a marketer, they may respond with: "My list will dwindle to ten people." Permission though is important. How do you balance permission with that double opt-in to maintain high deliverability? Make sure content is exactly the same across all brands. In essence, we throw a lot of best practices out the window because each business, program, piece of content is unique. From a list perspective, if somebody is telling you after three soft bounces to suppress that email address but you're only sending once a month, that is not a good strategy. We have to understand campaigns inside-out. If you read anything else about deliverability, it will simply describe "ten best practices," but that does not cut it from a business perspective. Or obtaining Paradise.

Marketers, since you've arrived at this point in our wild and wondrous Digital Age, I know you can master each of these nine layers and pass through content and technical gatekeepers alike:

1. Content
2. Lists
3. Bounces
4. Complaints
5. Spam Traps
6. Blacklists
7. Authentication
8. Compliance
9. Technology

Once you do, see you in Paradise!

First Challenge

Content

With a successfully delivered email, there are really three results you can expect: *deleted*, *read*, or *read and action taken*. Every business strives for the latter of those results. You not only want your email to be read, but you want the reader to take action: make the purchase, visit your store, sign up, etc.

Here are five ways to improve your email copywriting and write compelling content.

1. Be clear on your desired outcome.

Before you write anything, think first about your desired result. What are you hoping to accomplish with this email? Keeping that in mind, be sure that everything from the subject line to the content to the final call-to-action leads your recipient in the direction you desire.

2. Be friendly and personable.

Make sure the overall tone of your email is friendly and very personable. Your email will quickly stand out if you avoid the same, dry sales pitch approach as your competitors. If possible, personalize your email or even tailor and send to a particular segmented portion of your email list.

3. Align your subject line copy and email copy.

What your email subject line promises, the email message should deliver. When readers don't get what they're actually promised in the subject line, click-through rates will plummet—and in the long term, so will your email open rates.

4. Talk about benefits, not features.

You know the value of your email, but does your recipient? Not yet! And it's your job to explain it. Your email must explain the benefits of your offer to the reader.

5. Use actionable language.

That's right, emails have calls-to-action, too! Well, the good ones do. Beginning with the subject line, use language that makes it clear to the recipient what they can do with the information in the email should they choose to open it. Within the content of your email, the call-to-action should be extremely easy to identify. Remember, people scan their emails, and if there's one thing you want your recipient to pick up on, it's your call-to-action.

Remember, these tips can be applied regardless of your writing expertise. So the next time you send out marketing emails, keep these copywriting components in mind.

Subject Lines—Shocking, Funny, Simple, Mysterious

All of us in the email marketing space are jaded when it comes to receiving email from others. We know relevant subject lines, authenticated emails, segmentation—that is a large expectation from us. I think it is all about permission though that drives the psychological aspect. If I opted in and receive emails, my brain associates this with, *yes, I signed up for this, I needed this*. This happens at least once a day: I receive cold emails from brands I've never heard of and often, they're sending it to our generic email address and it strikes a chord. They're speaking to me like they know me, the subject line is surprising, and they are trying to sell to me in the first two sentences, but there are six paragraphs.

One of my majors in college was sociology. Essentially human beings will look at you and within the first five seconds, think they know everything about you. They'll start to build a profile on you in their head based upon race, age, gender, religion, hair color, hair length, clothing, eye color, glasses. Same thing with email. I've automatically built a profile on you if I don't know anything about you. The emails I receive better be permission-based, be responsive and carry a mobile-friendly design. Only then will I react. (Again, the actions are *delete*, *read* or *read and take action.*)

If you ask my mom, sister, or wife what kinds of email they actually open, the answer will differ. Some people like newsletters. Some, coupons. One great thing I applaud marketers for is offering opt-in. Going into a preference center, a portal for subscribers to manage their email preferences, and opting in is helpful. Optimize your preference page. Don't just have a one-click box. Drive them to social. If they are engaging on email, encourage them to follow on Facebook and Twitter. Giving people options keeps your brand top of mind, especially if they want to buy something from you.

Design and display are imperative. Litmus and Email on Acid are tools that determine what an email looks like on various platforms. You send an email to their software and they show you how it renders on platforms like mobile, tablet, B-to-B and B-to-C. Is it rendering properly? Too long? Getting cut off?

A few companies come up with subject line reports every year. They find that certain terms get higher clicks or lower clicks. B-to-C subject lines are typically short and to the point - "Fourth of July sale," "cruise alerts," "Groupon deals" - because people want to find out what the deal is. B-to-B subject lines are often longer because you need more detail. We have to look at the audience and how they will read it; we use those tools to see how long the subject line is before it's cut off.

The popular Xbox series, *Assassin's Creed Origins*, released a promo email, which was likely quite expensive in terms of time and people resources. Unfortunately, the subject line was so long, it cut off with "Ass." You'll commonly see bloopers like this. Subject lines gone wrong can hurt your brand. What words make the most sense for your category? If you're in the electronics business and sending B-to-B, the words, display and call-to-action should be considerably different than if targeting B-to-C.

People will tell me they are tired of content so broad and not focused that they don't read it. People will start to ignore your brand and they may not see the offer. From a deliverability perspective, over-sending will lead to list fatigue. No relevancy. If an email is over 102 kb in size, Gmail may clip it. At the bottom, it will say "message clipped; click here to view more."

One thing that is very popular are RSS feeds, blog feeds. A lot of companies take their RSS feed and turn it into an email and pull the blog information into smaller snippets. When a recipient clicks, that tells the mailbox provider that these recipients are interested in specific content. The marketer can then use that information to tailor subject lines in the future.

Today, email overload is a reality and grabbing someone's attention with a well-crafted subject line is more important than ever. In an effort to filter through irrelevant messages, most people spend just a few seconds glancing through subject lines to determine which emails to open.

The importance of subject lines becomes clear when you consider that the subject line of your email may be your first and only shot at connecting with a customer or business contact. Here are multiple tips for writing great subject lines that will help increase your open rates.

1. Personalize.

A subject line is the first impression that your prospect has of you. We all know first impressions last, so that is where personalization comes in handy. Studies by Marketing Sherpa and Pitney Bowes have concluded that Baby Boomers, Generation X, Millennials, and iGens in 2017 interact most with brands that use some sort of personalization in their communications. When speaking to someone using their name can be the sweetest sound to their ears. To imitate this with email, use effective personalization by adding {First-Name} and {Last-Name}, or even {Company-Name} into your subject line.

A study conducted by MailChimp showed that using a recipient's first and last name in the subject line had higher open rates than only using first *or* last name.

One vital best practice for personalization is understanding your prospect's buyer persona and where they are in the buyer's journey. Sending someone the wrong message at the wrong time will definitely not get opens and could potentially get them to mark your brand as "spam."

A 2015 study by Experian Marketing Services provided data that showed email subject lines that included the recipient's name increased open rates by 23.8 percent. Names are only one way to get higher open-rates. You can try using familiar language that implies a friendship, be casual, or share something personal.

2. Keep it brief.

Your subject line must quickly grab the recipient's attention. If this hasn't set in yet, think of your own Inbox. Take inventory. How many are sitting there because they made it in and didn't get dumped into inferno? In one snapshot from the subject lines, you know which one you want to open first.

You want to be very specific and descriptive in just a few short words. Studies show more people than ever are viewing email via a mobile device. With this trend, it's increasingly important to keep subject lines short and sweet because mobile devices display fewer characters of a subject line than their webmail and desktop counterparts. Because mobile email apps like the iPhone generally display around thirty-five characters of a subject line in the Inbox view, writing subject lines in the twenty- to forty-character range tends to be more effective.

3. Capture interest.

Subject lines need to be interesting and unique and communicate the promise of value. Your subject line should capture the recipient's attention and incentivize them to learn more by opening the email.

Alchemy Worx did a study from 24.5 billion subject lines, identifying "The Five Most Effective (and Ineffective) Words in Email Subject Lines." This study concluded which words had higher open rates and which words had the least effective open rates, with "upgrade" and "just" being the most opened, and "miss" and "deals" being the least opened.

In addition, Digital Marketer's study of "101 Best Email Subject Lines of 2016" analyzed 125 million subject lines and concluded that marketers should try using these phrases in their subject lines:

- ∞ "Get this now"
- ∞ "Is coming"

- (use numbers in your subject line) Example: "5-step plan," "3 week course," "101 ideas"

4. Ask recipients a question.

Questions provoke answers. When asking your recipients a question ask them about their pain points, business goals, personal goals, or questions that you would want answered if you were in their shoes. If you ask the right question, you will entice recipients of your email to click and therefore, have a high open rate subject line.

In Litmus' study on "How To Write The Perfect Subject Line," it was found that subject lines phrased as questions performed better than some similar messages phrased as statements.

5. Use greed factor.

You know the expression, "keeping up with the Joneses." What this expression means is that psychologically, everyone wants what everyone else has—even if that person isn't going to use the item. Again, knowing your audience is key to understanding their desires. Knowing your buyer persona is key.

Here are some example subject lines:

- Topshop: "Meet your new jeans"
- Topshop: "Get a head start on summer"
- HP: "Flash. Sale. Alert."
- HP: "New must-haves for your office"
- Seafolly: "A new product you won't pass on"
- Guess: "25% off your favorites"
- Rip Curl: "Two for two"
- La Mer: "A little luxury at a great price"
- Rapha: "Complimentary gift wrap on all purchases"
- The Black Tux: "Get priority access."

If a competitor is using key words, then automatically our curiosity or skepticism will get the best of us. We can use this strategy when developing our subject lines. It's also hard to pass up a good deal. Be careful, however, because if you give too high of a discount, most consumers will think the offer is fake.

6. Capitalize on fear of loss.

Maybe you have personally been enticed by a limited-time offer. Phrases like "don't want you to miss out," and "last day/week" emphasize a fear of loss. Feelings of urgency and scarcity are real! Studies show that subject lines with a time-sensitive appearance are proven to be seen as important and urgent. You can use this strategy in your subject lines by adding an element of scarcity (limited availability) or urgency (limited time).

7. Get creative with emojis and symbols. Go on, you know you want to.

Tempted to use the same symbols in your email subject lines as you do in impersonal text messages? You may want to because according to a study from Experian, using emojis in your subject line can increase your open rate by 45 percent. Be careful when choosing which emoji to use and make sure they are going to render properly on all mailbox providers. You don't want your subject line to have the ⊠ symbol. This symbol may trigger a spam filter and block you from Inbox placement.

8. Build trust.

There is nothing worse than opening an email with a catchy subject line, only to realize you have been tricked and that the email content is not consistent with the subject line topic. Trustworthiness is essential for marketing success, so always make sure that your email subject is relevant to the email content. In order to preserve credibility with your audience, it is also important that you review your subject line to determine that it is free of spelling or grammatical errors.

Finally, ask yourself, "Would I open this email?" Is it sufficiently compelling to stand out in your Inbox and generate a click? If not, keep working on it!

Battling for Attention with Pre-header Text

It doesn't matter if it's Gmail or an iPhone mail app, the very first line of your message can be read in the preview pane. This fifty-word description may not seem very important, but when your email subject line is less than perfect, this is another great way to tease your content and encourage readers to open your email. To get recipients hooked, make sure the first line of your message is as appealing as the opening line of a novel or screenplay.

Video Star?

Over 69 percent of marketers report using video in their marketing efforts. Cisco predicts that more than 84 percent of all Internet traffic will be video by 2018.

I have this argument with some of my team members. I'm Gen X. A lot of my employees are Millennials and like video. I like to read and comprehend instead. Personally, I think you should focus on content. Alternatively, looking at facts and data, people respond to video. They may not have time to read everything. Attention spans are a lot shorter since I was growing up. With the limited attention span, marketers need to focus on the preview pane—the golden rectangle. The first two seconds of reading an email is where you need to get your point across with call to action and conversion.

Gary Vaynerchuk, serial entrepreneur & motivational speaker, who often partners with Tony Robbins, focuses on how social media and video are creating additional entrepreneurs who have something to say. People will listen especially if you are giving them free content. They are watching videos and streaming through social media. I drive a lot of marketers and clients to understand that video is important and you should include it in your toolkit, but the fact that there is a video link in your email does not guarantee Inbox placement. People are probably watching the video while reading a tweet or doing something else.

Content is in the Eyes of the Beholder

With Google, you have to have a mobile-friendly website or it ranks you lower by default. This is all part of a formal 360 view of your entire email program. I expect that when I click on a link, it should send me to a mobile-optimized website or landing page. If I have to pinch and scroll and zoom, it is going to make me angry. I'm on a mobile device and you sent me a mobile-optimized email, but you didn't complete the 360 and send me to a mobilized landing page. Countless marketers miss this in 2017. In fact, so much that if we could take a peek into how many emails are lost in inferno, it would be a disgrace.

We're focused on a mobile-optimized society so give me the right landing page to go with it. Otherwise, I have to go back to my desk, laptop, pull that email up and then pull the link up again. If you are trying to sell me at the time of the email, sell me then with all the right components.

Test content on different platforms to make sure it renders properly on mobile device, tablet, Gmail. The worst thing is receiving an email from a brand and the CSS or images are broken. People will mark as spam because they think the brand has been phished or hacked. Review reports of data such as conversions and unsubscribes, and then use the data to do something different. It's all about adapting in this industry. Most people that are stagnant in this business are destroyed. Things change and evolve all the time. What worked last week probably won't work this week. Your readers expect something new and fresh. It's the marketer's job to give it to them and convert them to whatever it is they are selling. Subject lines, content, frequency—if you tell me I will receive one email a week, that is what I expect. For heaven's sake, when I sign up for a program, send me a welcome email. If you send it to me a week later, I will forget you. Welcome emails introduce me to your brand, set expectations, give me a coupon, let me know what your email is going to look like. Another no-no: never use no-reply@ in your from email address. That burns me up because if I am buying something from you and you send me a receipt with no-reply, it means buy from me but don't talk to me.

Clues of the Domain

One of the biggest tasks for marketers is making sure any domain you're sending from or a landing page or a tracking domain actually exists. You've probably seen this multiple times: links in the email that don't go back to the brand's website. Let's say Bed Bath and Beyond sent me an email and a link goes to Wine.com or a different brand; the problem is deliverability.

When content scanners are reading through your email, they are looking at every link. If the link has a bad reputation, it will affect your brand's deliverability. People don't realize this with their affiliates or third parties. We have worked with brands that have affiliates, third parties, and partners, and they will give them their lists. That affiliate is sending to problematic domains. It is using your domain to send that email. Reputation is so key when it comes to placement in multiple mailbox providers. You may have seen the info about DMARC, a third-party authentication that tries to protect the brand.

Anybody can boast, "Chris and his team helped me achieve better deliverability," but what are some of the specifics, such as data metrics and length of time the improvement took?

One of our large clients is a global online travel brand that sends millions of emails. With each email campaign needing to be approved by Legal before they can say things, there is much vulnerability when moving from one email service provider to another. Their contract expires, the service provider is too expensive, products are too limited, better products come out, and so forth, so they submit an RFP once a year or five years and then change providers. With a new service provider, you need to focus on creating a new domain name or keeping the same, and DNS will be different.

That strategy must include segmenting your list and eliminating contacts that are not active. You need people to "save" you, "star" you, "reply to" you, "mark" you as "not junk." Once we help with the migration to the platform, the client's open rate goes down. You have to watch unsubscribes and bounces and then migrate them to the new platform. If you do not, you will send recipients to a lot of invalids and people who have marked you as spam, which could negatively affect your reputation. They will have a dedicated account manager that helps you go through a checklist.

Congratulations, you've ascended to the second challenge—lists!

Second Challenge

Lists

Would you send a love letter to your kindergarten teacher? A steakhouse coupon to a vegan? Lists and segmentation are extremely important. Are you sending to people that opted in? Are you sending to people that have recently opened and clicked? Is this a master list in which you haven't done any sort of segmentation? This is very problematic.

Which of the following have the biggest impact on improving the likelihood of emails reaching the inbox (i.e deliverability)?

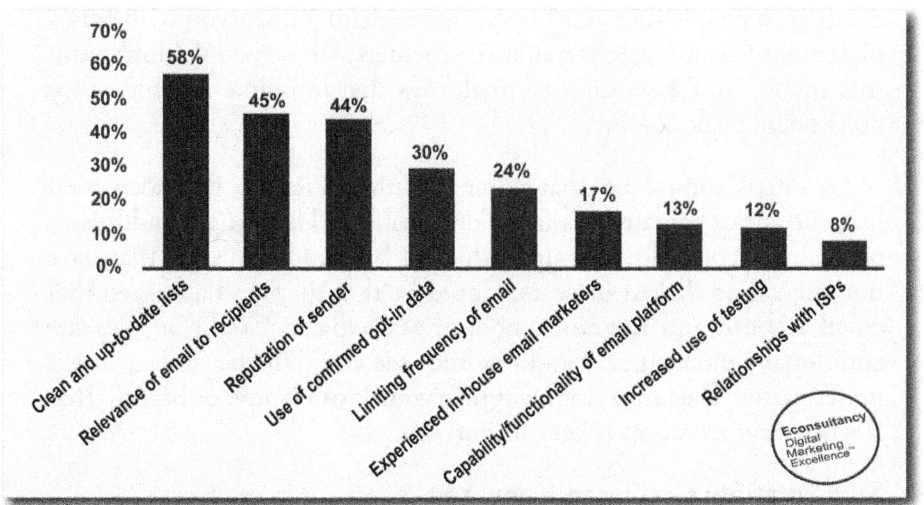

Figure 6. Biggest Impact on Deliverability (Source: Econsultancy)

Brands will often use the same IP and same domain to send out multiple segments to people who should be segmented by IP and domain. Example: If you are a brand sending out bulk emails or newsletters, but you're also sending out receipts, those need to be separated by IP and/or subdomain. One of the reasons is that if your bulk email goes in the junk folder, your transactional and receipts may also go into junk. Firewalling and segmenting off different mail streams, different brands underneath one big brand, will help you monitor or review any sort of reputational problems that you have.

For instance, you're on a blacklist and if you use the same IP or domain, your corporate domain can be on a blacklist. Large companies will use their corporate email domain to send out marketing communications. Great from a branding perspective, but from a technical and deliverability perspective, it's horrible.

No. 1, you want to use a subdomain so in case something happens, it won't affect your top-level or corporate email domain. Example: news.homedepot.com, update.cocacola.com. It allows you to firewall or segment you away from your corporate domain. That is very important.

The list can have major deliverability problems. The list is old. The list is purchased. The list was scraped. The list isn't segmented. Sending to people that aren't opening or clicking hurts you with Inbox placement because it tells mailbox providers, "these people don't want this email." You're sending to mailboxes that look like zombies; they don't open, click, log in!

A lot of companies that come to Inbox Pros do not keep their lists current or update it as far as engagement. Updating an address is one thing. People do keep up with a list but send to people that have not opened or clicked in years. Could be that they've abandoned that email account and therefore, nobody is seeing it. Could be they are emotionally unengaged. Could be they see you, but the subject line is not enticing. They may not recognize your From Name or brand. That is where segmentation is very important.

Segmentation: Getting to Know You

Segmenting by activity and by demographics helps to get into the Inbox. If I am sending to recent openers and clickers, I have a greater chance of getting in the Inbox. If that is a part of my segmentation, but I also include time zone, preference, demographics and make it known that my content goes along with such, I am going to have a higher engagement overall than sending a blanket email off to everybody and calling it a day.

That is where segmentation is very important. The B-to-B senders tend to do a lot of lead acquisition and buying leads. A lot of the B-to-C senders are focused on driving traffic to their site, coupons, discounts, social. They are trying to get consumers on Hotmail, Yahoo!, and Gmail engaged. When you open a new company and want to try and drive sales, some marketers believe that the only way to get sales is to buy a list. Major brands like Home Depot, Bed, Bath and Beyond are well-known and use other channels.

Confession: I actually bought a list of 4 million emails for $20 as an experiment to see what would happen. The emails were like aaa123@yahoo.com and other clearly made up email addresses. If I were to send to them, the majority would hard bounce. There's no way that many people would have this kind of account. The number of hard bounces would get me blocked and cause problems with my brand's deliverability.

Since segmentation can allow for personalization, what is the best segment info to pinpoint when forming lists? Is geographic targeting still helpful? If available, historical data such as site logins & conversions is great for segmentation. That way, you know who your five-star people are. When you look at things like demographics, you can look at regional location to optimize 8:00 on Monday morning or 4:00 on Thursday.

Another effective technique is to use buyer segment—someone just interested in a particular product, who is also interested in a coupon versus newsletter. This information lets you know what people will open a certain email versus ignore it. I've been on multiple calls in the past week, which have shown that age is still a key demographic just based upon the fact that certain people buy versus complain about email. One brand I've been talking to caters to an older demographic. The users are notorious for hitting the "spam" or "unsubscribe" button.

Let's say you are a business owner that buys a $50,000 X-ray machine. This happens all the time for car dealerships and mortgage lenders. You don't buy these things every day. That is a key point for list segmentation. Knowing the product, knowing your buyer and what they are interested in. Let's say you are a mortgage company with a long list of customers. You might be tempted to partner up with someone who can use that list; they can market homeowner's insurance or something related to that big product. That can get you in trouble though because people may not opt-in to receive emails from all these third parties. People that use AOL may hit the "spam" button and that is how they "unsubscribe." For them, AOL is a different experience than Gmail. If you are a product or brand promoting to older generations, you may receive more spam complaints.

Attraction to Analytics

Advanced analytics software providers help users peer through a window of their campaign to see subscriber activity patterns and mobile view stats. A lot of companies are focused on email analytics and optimization. While metrics are important in understanding things like tracking, the best times to send, best times to open, they do not guarantee Inbox placement. You can have all these fancy tools and software, but if your emails aren't reaching Inboxes, you're wasting money. It is a combination of doing the right things to get in the Inbox and lead to conversion. Marketers are focused too often on opens and clicks. If I were running a marketing department, my focus would be on conversions.

Why are people unsubscribing? Wrong message or are we sending too often? What is a favorable response time (click, call to action) before considering an email campaign unsuccessful? I get these questions all the time. Should I remove people if they haven't opened in a certain time? Maybe people have abandoned that email box. We don't want to get rid of people because maybe they want to open quicker. It may have gone straight to the junk folder because of poor practices and no one will ever see it. If someone has not opened and clicked in twelve months or six months, it may be time to "remove." In truth, there is no one-size-fits-all for getting rid of people or calling a campaign unsuccessful.

Double Opt-In: Where Open Rates Soar

When it comes to email marketing, companies and organizations are faced with a choice. "Do we use double opt-in or single opt-in when acquiring new email subscribers?" Ultimately, email senders have to choose between list size and list quality.

A popular form of opt-in is called the single opt-in, in which the user agrees to receive an email by simply checking a box, or leaving a pre-checked box checked, or entering their email address when they visit a website. Upon submission, the subscriber immediately begins receiving marketing emails. With this form of opt-in people are prone to forget they "asked" to be emailed in the first place and can mark your message as spam. This form of opt-in tends to generate more bounces, blacklisting, spam trap hits, and other nasty stuff that can adversely affect your deliverability rates.

With double opt-in, a new email subscriber signs up on your site and provides their email address, but in order to receive your email messages, they must confirm their approval by actually acknowledging your very first email to them. They are not officially subscribed until they click a link in the first confirmation email. While this extra step can result in fewer opt-ins than single opt-ins purely in terms of the number of subscribers, double opt-ins are superior for *all* other stats. It's not the size of your list that counts; it is the overall quality.

Will using double opt-in really improve the stats that matter: opens, clicks, bounces, and unsubscribes?

If you're planning to build long-term email marketing success, you need quality subscribers much more than you need *quantity*. Therefore, confirmed emails are much more valuable than the unconfirmed emails of single opt-in. If the extra step is too much trouble for a subscriber, then they were not likely a good fit in the first place.

When it comes to stats, deliverability rates for lists that use double opt-in are significantly higher, unsubscribe rates are lower and open and click through rates are higher as well.

Essentially, it boils down to this: double opt-in is a long-term strategy with a ton of long-term benefits. It generally increases deliverability rates, open rates, and click-through rates. Your email marketing results will soar when you focus on building a list of engaged email subscribers rather than merely looking for short-term success.

Dynamic, Real-Time Automation

Incorporating automation into your email marketing efforts is an excellent way to develop your customer relationships through regular contact. Automated emails are pre-written emails sent over timed intervals in a series, triggered by a certain customer behavior. By setting up campaigns to send out emails on time-based intervals, you are increasing consumer touch points, and if done well, you can begin to build trust with your customer.

Automated emails deliver information to your customers right when they need it, in a way that's efficient for you and your team. Send a series of emails, to build rapport, increase your company familiarity and nurture leads.

The idea is simple. By continuously interacting via a touch point, the recipient will warm towards whatever the eventual end goal is. That could be a sale, a sign-up or even simply engagement on a social media page. These are all great examples of what an automated email marketing campaign can do.

Here are scenarios in which automated emails could be used most effectively:

- When a subscriber signs up for your list
- Birthday or anniversary
- Follow-up to website activity
- Thanking your customer
- Following up after a purchase
- Soliciting feedback on a new product or service
- Tips or other education
- Renewal reminders
- Product instructions
- Coupons and promotions

Test and Test Again

Most email marketing providers allow you to A/B split test for your email campaigns. In other words, you can send out two emails with different subject lines and see which one was opened more. You can also test different calls-to-action, types of messages and other factors such as time of day to see if you receive higher open rates.

Since content and lists provide the infrastructure for your email campaigns, and sometimes communication platform as a whole, here are tips for mastering lists:

1. You're probably not alone on your IP address.

Since the volume of email sent by B-to-B marketers is often much lower than retailers or other B-to-C sites, marketing automation providers often spread the usage of their email IP addresses across multiple clients. As a matter of fact, most marketing automation subscriptions default to a shared IP. Consider checking with your provider on the costs associated with a dedicated IP address for your company; otherwise, your deliverability could be impacted by the bad practices of the other companies on the same IP.

2. More volume is not always better.

Major B-to-C mailbox providers typically publish the volumes that they accept on an hourly basis. Unfortunately, B-to-B senders don't receive that information. Many B-to-B networks and mail servers can handle small volumes and don't have dedicated mail server administrators. This makes it difficult to send a large amount of volume to these B-to-B networks. Instead, send smaller volumes and spread out the volume over the course of your send to achieve better results.

3. Not everyone likes to talk to strangers.

Keeping a clean, active email list is key to achieving high deliverability. Meticulously manage your lists by removing unsubscribes, suppressing complaints, coming up with a good bounce strategy, and using caution with list append and acquisition providers. Strive to continually segment and prune email lists to get the results you want and get into the Inbox.

4. Suppress those that complain.

B-to-B feedback loops exist and should be set up and enabled for your email programs. A feedback loop allows the recipient's network to send you back email digests of those that complain (i.e. hitting the "spam" button) about your emails. Not all networks/providers have this, but it is important to sign up for all that are available, as well as suppress those that do complain.

5. Stay safe with whitelisting.

Whitelisting, or safe-listing, has long been associated with B-to-C mailers. The truth is that getting your recipients to whitelist your sending IP address(es) and sending domain(s) to their mail server and/or mail-filtering solution will help improve deliverability. Often, marketing emails will get quarantined on the mail server but by having your sending information whitelisted, your emails will bypass this and get delivered to your recipient. Always include this information in your emails, on your website, and communicate this to your recipients.

6. Provide your passport to the Inbox.

IP and domain authentication are very important when sending B-to-B emails. Setting up these two types of authentication is typically simple to do and helps your deliverability. By enabling IP and domain authentication for your email programs, you are showing your passport to your recipient's network and stating, "I am who I say I am." This helps your recipient's network possibly filter out any emails that are not authenticated and could be spam.

7. URLs may not be your friend.

Content URLs can also pose deliverability challenges. As IPs can get blacklisted, so can domains and URLs. Make sure you test all URLs, not only to make sure that they work, but also check to see if they are blacklisted. Too many URLs could also potentially cause deliverability problems, so always plan on testing when doing your content checks. Avoid using URL shorteners, as many of those are blacklisted, and make sure that the domains you are referencing don't keep redirecting to many other URLs.

8. Pay attention to reporting and analytics.

Deliverability reporting is not glamorous, but paying attention to it will help improve conversions and revenue. Don't just focus on opens, clicks, and conversions, but pay close attention to bounces, unsubscribes, and complaints from your lists. Keeping an eye out for IP and domain reputation is very important as well. Staying off blacklists, monitoring blocks, and reviewing deliverability data/reports will help make sure that you maintain high deliverability.

Marketers must have a consistent and proactive approach to email deliverability to run programs that drive revenue.

Voices of Deliverability

Michael Ballard, Sr. Manager, Digital Marketing, Commercial Marketing, Lenovo North America

How has deliverability changed the way that you send email within your organization (content, lists, technology, etc.)?

We are very sensitive to not only the technical email components (text, headers, html, etc.) but also, our messaging. We are constantly trying to find the balance between creativity and spam filters. Being edgy, but not too edgy.

How do you anticipate deliverability will change for your organization in the next decade?

I believe the days of "mass blast emails" will go away and be replaced with one-to-one emails only.

Do you actively segment out inactive recipients that could affect Inbox placement? If so, how often do you segment out these in-actives?

We still talk to those people. However, we report on them separately.

Congratulations, you've ascended to the third challenge—bounces!

Third Challenge

Bounces

Many of us don't like the moniker, "failure," but a hard bounce is a permanent delivery failure. Some reasons for a hard bounce would be sending to a mailbox that doesn't exist (bad mailbox) or a domain that doesn't exist (bad domain). Mailbox providers monitor and watch for IP addresses that continually send to bad mailboxes and get blocked due to complaints—and they will adjust your IP/domain reputation accordingly.

Maintain a bounce rate of less than 5 percent, as recommended by most major mailbox providers. The lower the number of hard bounces you receive, the better your reputation with networks. It's important that maintain a clean email list by removing undeliverable email addresses from your list on a consistent basis.

What's the difference between a soft bounce and a hard bounce? Yes, both are bounces! A bounce is from an email being rejected by a recipient's mail server. However, there are several different reasons why your emails could be bouncing. It could range from the recipient's mailbox being full to the domain name not existing. So what differentiates them? One is permanent and the other is not. It is highly suggested to pay attention to your bounce logs as your deliverability reputation can be impacted.

The lighter of the two, a *soft bounce*, is an email that reached the recipient's mail server but bounced back before it made it to the recipient. Soft bounces could be caused by a recipient's mailbox being full, the email server being offline or rate-limiting the number of messages it receives, or the message itself being too large. If a contact soft bounces for multiple campaigns, it is best to suppress the email address entirely.

Soft bounces often result from:

- ∞ Full mailbox
- ∞ ISP block
- ∞ Blacklist
- ∞ Offline or rate-limiting mail server
- ∞ Your message is too large

In any of these cases, retry the email at a proper interval, then suppress for that campaign. Retry for the next few campaigns (analyze the bounce details) and if it still doesn't deliver, stop sending to the contact.

Hard bounces are emails that have been returned to the sender because there has been a permanent failure, which means retrying won't change the outcome. These will negatively affect your email deliverability. Some of the more common hard bounces are the recipient's address being invalid, the domain name not existing, or the receiving server blocking delivery from your domain or IP address. Hard bounces can, therefore, be a result of a poor sending reputation, as well as causing a poor reputation if they are sent unchecked.

Hard bounces often result from:

- ∞ The email doesn't exist
- ∞ The domain name doesn't exist
- ∞ Your recipient's email server has blocked your emails

In any of these cases, immediately stop sending to the contact. Analyze the most common bounces to determine the source of the bad addresses.

Knowing the difference between a soft bounce and a hard bounce is crucial when trying to put focus on needed email deliverability efforts.

A significant percentage of hard bounces is an indicator of an unhealthy list, so pay special attention to those and take action to analyze your list and clean where it's needed.

Bounce Rates Jam Traffic

Pay close attention to each campaign's bounce rate, specifically the hard bounces and the soft bounces. The hard bounce rate will let you know the amount of invalid email addresses and bad domains that you are sending to. Most platforms will suppress these bounces so you will not send to them again. The soft bounce rate is a temporary bounce, but can continue to cause issues that may be related to IP/domain reputation issues. Monitoring and reviewing the details of these bounces will let you know if your campaigns are blocked at a particular network, possibly blacklisted, or being deferred because of reputation issues.

Monitoring hard and soft bounces from a given domain and IP are a primary way ISPs gain insight into a sender's list practices and therefore, make quality judgments about whether or not the sender is a spammer or abusive marketer.

Regularly monitoring both hard and soft bounces is strongly recommended, as it not only provides a window into how ISPs view a sender's marketing email program, it can also contain the very first indications of systemic problems with opt-in and list acquisition. Additionally, bounce logs provide the first signs that ISPs have begun to view the sender's email program poorly and if the reputation issues are not addressed, deliverability impacts will follow.

Many ISPs will only accept emails at certain rates correlated with the sending IP and/or domain's reputation at that ISP. That is to say if a sender's reputation drops at a particular ISP, the ISP will begin to rate limit that sender. It is vital to regularly identify rate limiting in the bounce logs for exactly that reason: they are often the first sign a sender has that their reputation is poor. If rate limiting bounces are ignored, the reputation may continue to drop, unnoticed, until it is low enough to cause significant deliverability problems and to require significant time and effort to repair. These bounces may be sent initially as soft bounces, and then the ISP may choose to make the bounces permanent if the issue is ignored. Eventually, the ISP may choose to filter or even block the sender completely.

Another category of bounces is "spammy" content, meaning that the email was rejected by a content filter. This is a deceptive category because marketers often think of spam filters as formulae, in which the right email design is admitted and the wrong one is rejected. In fact, modern spam filters are learning algorithms that not only look for spam triggers in the email content, but also examine authentication and their users' reactions to the email. The conclusion is that "spam-like content" actually often means "users didn't engage with it" and that may be less to do with the actual content and more to do with the sending infrastructure and also with the users receiving it, and therefore, whether or not they actually wanted it or even expected it.

Abandoned and overfilled mailboxes means exactly what it sounds like: the user is not monitoring the mailbox and it has filled up its allotted space on the recipient server. When a user changes jobs, their email address may not be deactivated for some time, causing it to fill up and indicate to the ISP or IT team that the senders filling it are not paying attention to engagement or auto-responders.

Reputation blocking is another type of bounce category, indicating simply that the recipient ISP/network does not trust the sender. This can be caused by many things, including authentication, grey-listing, blacklisting, third-party reputation sites, and more.

Again, It's Your Reputation!

Bounce rates affect your reputation on your IP address. If your bounce rates are too high, the ISP may think you are trying to spam them and block your domain or IP address. There is no "magic number" that can get you blocked/bulked. List management is crucial and marketers should scrub lists regularly to remove the hard and soft bounces.

If you sent the same message twice and it didn't get blocked the first time, there are many reasons why this could have occurred:

- ∞ Did you send to a new list that you haven't sent to before?
- ∞ Did you receive a lot of abuse complaints/hit a lot of spam traps?
- ∞ Has the reputation of the IP address gone down?

ISPs can and will change their filters thousands of times a day. A word/phrase that was accepted two hours ago may be blocked now. Test your content before sending to your live lists.

Besides content being the culprit, there is a high likelihood that you could have deliverability issues if you change your *from* domain. Here are some reasons:

- ∞ Your new *from* domain is not set up with the proper authentication and brand protection (SPF, DKIM, DMARC).
- ∞ Your subscribers have already whitelisted your *from* domain with their internal filtering systems. If so, your email may go to the bulk folder.
- ∞ Your subscribers may not recognize you and they may be more likely to click the *abuse* button.

There are many ways to reduce the number of abuse complaints:

- ∞ Only send to those recipients that signed up. Never purchase lists!
- ∞ Don't send to those recipients who have asked to be removed from your list.
- ∞ Don't send to old lists. These recipients may not remember signing up and complain.
- ∞ Send relevant content to your subscribers.
- ∞ Personalize your content with subject lines.
- ∞ Add an opt-out link to the top of your email. This will allow those users who may not know where the opt-out link is to find out and opt-out versus complain.
- ∞ Separate promotional and transactional IPs and domains.

Congratulations, you've ascended to the fourth challenge—complaints!

Fourth Challenge

Complaints

People always ask, what part of deliverability is most important? If you have low bounces, low complaints, high clicks and opens, you can be edgier with your content. Best Buy sends an email weekly of one giant image. This is usually a no-no because no one can see it unless they download the image. There is no text, but they have a good reputation and high opens/clicks.

It's a balance. If the mailbox provider expects a certain email volume and they don't get it, something is up. If they get more, something is up. I always tell marketers and brands to set the expectations not just with recipients but also with the mailbox providers. Don't just send more volume overnight. Customers may think someone hacked your account.

It's 2017, and a lot of these decisions are being made by machines. These spam filters are looking at data points. Humans are on the other side making updates and monitoring and helping as needed. Multiple add-ons are available to purchase so you can tailor your messaging. If you are traveling, maybe your email will be tailored to the locale you're in or based on the time you usually open and click on email.

I saw a great picture the other day that said in 1997, "do not talk to strangers, do not give your information to strangers, do not get in the car with strangers."

In 2017, companies like Uber and Airbnb and other companies for convenience encourage you to give up data and your privacy. They watch where you are going and how often you are going to tailor information to you. We live in a world where two of the most valuable companies in the world own nothing, Uber and Airbnb, they have an app. They're not Microsoft or Oracle. Last time I checked the valuation of Uber, they were hovering around $60 billion. All that information, all that data, helps marketers customize the message to you and when to send it so it does not sit there. Plug-ins will show you the weather and traffic where you're currently at, along with personal interests.

Remember all the early rules? "Tuesday at 9:00 is the best time to send messages." "Never send on Friday." These rules have changed. We're an always-on society. But tailor the messages to me personally so I'm interested in what you're selling.

Sorry, but Unsubscribe Me...Now!

A good unsubscribe page makes it easy to unsubscribe and hard to want to. Preference pages are helpful for recipients to opt-down versus opt-out. First, however, know the essentials before treating it as a pesky add-on. It is better to get an unsubscribe than a spam complaint.

We know you don't want people to unsubscribe from your brand. That's why you may have thought it'd be clever to make it a maze for your users to unsubscribe. A lot of people think this tactic will make the other person impatient and forget about it, but they don't. Your average user is going to get irritated and click "spam" because the button is easy to find.

Why is this bad? If the ratio of spam complaints to clicks gets too high, mailbox providers will filter your messages to the spam folder and may even block you. Your complaint rate should always stay below 0.3% with a target rate of below 0.1%.

The goal isn't to keep as many subscribers as possible. It's to turn your subscribers into conversions. If someone wants to unsubscribe, they aren't going to convert, so it's best to just let them go.

What happens? If you make it difficult for a user to unsubscribe, they'll flag your email as spam. Everyone knows where the "spam" button is.

Don't get discouraged. Again, an unsubscribe page is a landing page. Therefore, it's another opportunity to spark the interest that led to the subscription in the first place. This page is where marketers can shine with creative opt-ins and valuable incentives.

Also, it's a perfect opportunity to find out what your subscriber actually cares about! You can provide options and different pitches: maybe the mail was just too frequent, or maybe they were hoping for different content than you were sending? Another tactic you could use is offering feedback forms next to the unsubscribe button. This is an opportunity to learn what needs improvement. You can test different re-opt-in content on the unsubscribe page as well. If an offering or incentive is enough to change the mind of an abandoning user, you know you've got something good!

Different actions for an unsubscribe page are:

- ∞ Change frequency of newsletters
- ∞ Change the content sent
- ∞ Offer short feedback forums
- ∞ Test different re-opt in content

Many companies have used unsubscribe pages to their advantage.

For example, Groupon sent more than 70,000 emails. 740 users reached the preferences page where they viewed a video showing Groupon's good intentions and their offerings to reinforce their message of select deals. Only 100 actually decided to unsubscribe after all. That means 85 percent of people who initially wanted to unsubscribe were retained at the unsubscribe page.

Your unsubscribe process should be simple and take effect immediately. It's better to lose a subscriber than gain a spam complaint. When designing the landing page, keep in mind that subscribers won't remember your facts and figures but will remember how you made them feel.

Keeping IP(s) Warm?

What is the difference between a dedicated IP and shared IP? How do I know which one I should be using? If this sounds like you, you've come to the right place. There are several factors that come into play when deciding whether to use a dedicated or shared IP with your business.

A dedicated IP address is unique to the sender. No other company, organization, or individual can send from that IP address other than your brand. Many think they should move to a dedicated IP address because they won't be affected by other senders and will be in charge of their reputation. This is a common misconception. Dedicated IP addresses are not always the answer.

We recommend that senders should only move to a dedicated IP address if:

∞ You are a higher-volume sender. Each ESP is different on how they view a 'higher volume sender,' but we recommend a minimum of 500,000 emails per month.

∞ You have the volume to be on a dedicated IP address and other users on the shared IP address are affecting your reputation and Inbox placement. This also includes blacklists and spam traps.

∞ You are prepared to pay for your dedicated IP address, and depending on the ESP (Email Service Provider), it could be a couple thousand dollars (or more)!

A shared IP address is shared by multiple senders…hence the name! For example, if you send emails through HubSpot without a dedicated IP address then your emails will be sent using the same IP as other HubSpot senders.

While a shared IP address may be good for your brand because you are a smaller volume sender, you are still sharing your reputation with other users. ESPs understand this and will try to put your brand in an IP pool with other similar senders.

Always ask your ESP about the other users in your sending pool. Just like elementary school, one bad egg can ruin things for everyone else. A bad sender in your pool can negatively impact your sending infrastructure as well.

Shared IP addresses are more cost effective than dedicated IP addresses. It's important to monitor each IP address your brand uses as each can affect deliverability differently. A big factor depends on the reputation of each IP address.

With a dedicated IP address, you are solely responsible for your reputation. Think of it like the first day of high school. First impressions are everything, and if you make one mistake (using a bad link in an email, not following proper warm-up practices, etc.), it will follow you for a while. This means if you do something to hurt your reputation with the mailbox providers, it will take time for them to regain their trust in you as a sender. This in turn will affect Inbox placement and deliverability.

If your IP address lands on a blacklist or hits a large amount of spam traps, you'll know that it's nobody else's fault except your own. From there you can try to figure out what caused the spam trap hits.

Your sending reputation is a critical deciding factor in whether a mailbox provider will deliver the message to the Inbox or not. A dedicated IP address is easier to whitelist (Identifying you as a 'safe sender.' You pass through spam filters a lot easier than someone who isn't whitelisted). For example, asking AOL to whitelist your dedicated IP address will increase your chances of an approval, versus a sender who has multiple shared IP addresses asking the same thing. Even if you get whitelisted, it's not permanent. You can always be removed based off of your sending practices.

Another way using a dedicated IP can affect your deliverability is from sole ownership in DNS records. DNS records point right back to your brand. For example, if you were to do a reverse DNS lookup on a dedicated IP address, it would have information that is associated with your brand only.

If your IP address lands on a blacklist or hits a large amount of spam traps, you'll know that it's nobody else's fault except your own. From there you can try to figure out what caused the spam trap hits.

There are a variety of solutions to increasing your reputation. Even if you've landed on a blacklist, each blacklist filters differently. After you figure out the problem, avoid making the same mistakes in the future as both blacklists and spam traps have an effect on your deliverability—which you are solely responsible for. A dedicated IP is easier to whitelist. Also, you possess sole ownership in DNS records.

With a shared IP, you are sharing your reputation. Just like the dedicated description, this can be a good or bad thing. This depends on what type of sender you are, what type of IP pool you are in, and what type of sender those other brands are that are sharing the IP address. While a shared IP address is more cost effective, your chances of hitting more spam traps and blacklists increase with the amount of companies using the IP address.

It is difficult to whitelist a shared IP address. A mailbox provider could be nervous and say no to a shared IP address because there are multiple senders using the IP address. This then means you'll have a harder time passing the spam filters versus a user that's whitelisted. DNS records don't point back to just your company. Due to being in a shared division, the DNS records are grouped.

If you are a lower-volume sender, a shared IP address may be just right for your company because you won't have to worry about the amount of spam trap hits versus your reputation plummeting because of the hits.

When deciding whether a shared or dedicated IP address is right for you, first look at the total volume of emails you send a month. Then ask yourself is it worth getting a dedicated IP address? Factor in the cost of having a dedicated IP. Look at your content and how you acquire your email lists. If you don't follow best practices, you will have to start because there's nowhere to hide with a dedicated IP address. Weigh out the pros and cons of both a shared and dedicated IP address. If a shared IP is right for you, do research on the IP pool you are in and how your ESP groups their users.

You should choose a dedicated IP if you have a 'high sending volume,' want to be in control of how your reputation develops, have sole responsibility in your DNS records, and have a larger budget. For a shared IP, you must be okay sharing your reputation with a group. It's always smart to research the group you are in because your chances of hitting more spam traps and blacklists increase with the amount of companies using the IP address. It will be harder to whitelist a shared IP, and DNS records don't point back to just your company. However, this may be the better option if you have a smaller budget. Whichever you decide to choose, make sure to factor in all the variables above. This one decision can have a large impact on your reputation with mailbox providers!

Marketers are often confused about the point of IP and Domain warming: "Everything is authenticated and I'm not using a blacklisted IP, so what's the problem?" In short: senders who blast to their entire list without history look like spammers.

These mailbox providers can choose what to accept or reject, and they want to protect their users from spammers who just want to make a quick buck and then disappear, so marketers have to distinguish themselves from those spammers.

To see the perspective of their spam filter, imagine for a moment that you're a Castle Gatekeeper in Medieval Europe. You need to let vendors (emails) into the castle every day but keep out trash that nobody wants (spam) and worse: con men.

A huge cart rolls up: you've seen this vendor (domain) before and know that he usually goes home with an empty cart (opened emails): your castle wants his stuff. You check the content, you check his papers (authentication), he's from a town (IP) with a good reputation, and all is in order so you let him in.

Now comes another cart full of emails that look alright, but you've never seen this domain before. Does your castle even want them? This IP has never sent from this domain before and for all you know he's trying to make a quick buck cheating the townsfolk. What do you do with the second cart?

- Turn him away flat?
- Let him bring in only a few emails to see if they get a positive response?
- Put him in the spam corner to see if anyone looks for him?
- Some combination of the above?

No matter what you do, you'll remember him as the guy who appeared without warning and tried to bring in his massive haul of unknown emails from an unknown place. Not the behavior of a trustworthy medieval market vendor!

Now let's turn it around: you're a medieval market vendor and you've just set up in a new town and gotten new papers. You know your emails are high quality and that the castle-dwellers will appreciate them. How do you convince the gatekeeper to let you in and form a profitable relationship?

Just showing up uninvited from a new IP with ten tons of emails is going to convince the gatekeeper that you're there to spam and disappear. Show your good intentions: bring only a mule-load, emails you know are wanted because they're addressed to people who've opened before. The gatekeeper will see your papers, your good content, and that you aren't bringing enough to profitably spam, and will let you in. Then, when people open your mail, the Gatekeeper will notice.

That doesn't mean show up with your ten-ton cart tomorrow, the Gatekeeper has only known you for a day!

Bring another small load of emails you know will be opened. Work your volume up so that each day the Gatekeeper notices you're getting good opens and clicks and people aren't complaining.

Finally, you've worked your way up to your ten-ton cart, and the Gatekeeper waves you right in with confidence while rejecting a brash new vendor who tried to send to his whole list at once with no history.

Whenever you change Towns (IP addresses) or Seller's Marks (Domains) or have new Papers (SPF and DKIM Authentication), the Gatekeeper (Spam Filter) is going to be suspicious. In a very real sense, you look like a different sender and have to prove again that you intend to be a responsible sender with desired content and practices that don't harm the users of the Castle.

To do this, you "warm" your IP or Domain by starting with mule-loads: maybe a few dozen messages sent to each mailbox provider. Make sure the messages go to users who are likely to engage: use recent click and open data. Send more the next day, and so on, until you have grown smoothly to your target volume. To ensure proper warming is taking place, you must put your best foot forward, and begin to send to your "best addresses" first. This means that you will begin the IP warming plan by sending to your most engaged users first. This will improve email delivery up front. As the warming plan continues, you will move from most engaged, to engaged, to somewhat engaged, and will end the warming period with your least engaged users. A successful ramp-up will increase your email delivery. As you continue each day of the warming period (note: the amount of days involved in the warming period will depend on the size of your email list), you will gradually add more addresses. For example, Day One, you may send to 500 email address and Day Two, you will send to 750. You can expect that Day Three will increase from Day Two.

IP warming may seem tedious and long; however, if you don't follow all the best practices and necessary steps, you have the potential to look like a spammer to mailbox providers and not increase email delivery. It's typical of a spammer to use and abuse an IP address and then move on to another IP. Email deliverability best practices are to do an IP warming plan when a new dedicated IP address is made and put your best foot forward to show mailbox providers that you are not spammers.

If your IP is not or has never been on a warming plan, your mail may be getting sent to spam, consistently lowering your reputation with mailbox providers and eventually (hopefully not) getting yourself marked on a blacklist.

All these issues can be avoided if you have an IP warming plan. Whether you are starting a new dedicated IP or remediating deliverability issues in the past, starting an IP warming plan will increase email delivery for you.

You may have a disadvantage if your new IP had spammers on it in the past and is starting out untrusted. Also, if you're leaving an abusive IP, the bad reputation may partially stick to the domain. This is where many senders make mistakes: they use a one-size-fits-all warming plan when there isn't one.

What one mailbox provider wants to see is significantly different from another. The experience and industry connections necessary to stay up-to-date on topics like these don't form overnight, so it's vital to make sure you've talked to an expert before you inadvertently ruin your reputation with your first campaign.

With IP warming, you want to start with a slow volume, use your best emails first and then ramp up over time. You get to reinvent yourself. People may be in a hurry and panicked, may have gotten kicked off their first server. Your bounce rate will be high and your reputation low, then you have to start over. Most of these systems are automated in a way to identify you based on a variety of metrics. Things like reputation, volume, content, complaints and bounces, and spam traps. Mailbox providers look and grade you just like teachers. What kind of grade? Good, bad, neutral, or not enough information. When we work with a client, we will introduce ourselves to a mailbox provider to request a block removal. Having that open conversation and education from them is important. They know what they want you to do. Will you adhere to it? We've worked with clients that didn't follow the plan. Then they're on their own.

People equate deliverability with fitness. The trainer tells you what to do to lose weight, gain muscle strength, but you don't care and eat burgers and drink beer all day. Same thing in our space. I watch *The Profit*. He took one company from $750,000 to $10 million in less than three years. He said, "this happens when you follow the process." I'm taking you from Purgatory to Paradise, and this is the plan to stick to. Clients see benefits when they do their part. A client came to us with bad Gmail problems. They followed the plan and a couple weeks later, they saw improvements. It's about assessing, putting a plan together and then following through.

Voices of Deliverability Inferno

Asher Amiel, Sr. Email Technical Support Analyst, RentPath

How has deliverability changed the way that you send email within your organization (content, lists, technology, etc.)?

Since we want to ensure subscribers open and click through our emails, we target subscribers we know will have a positive engagement when receiving our emails. We accomplished this by sending emails that have relevant content to our target subscribers, ensure there is a prominent unsubscribe link so subscribers can opt-out and we maintain a clean subscriber list on a regular basis.

What's the one thing you would change in the deliverability space to help improve your job and/or improve Inbox placement?

The receiving systems availability. Because sending servers queue messages over an amount of time, if the receiving server is not available, the message could be delivered but if the recipient's mailbox is not available (anything could happen, such as server offline or unavailable, etc.), the receiving server could hold messages and make attempts to deliver but if unsuccessful it could bounce. The ideal situation would be if the sending and receiving server understood something was offline/unavailable and just hold it until it came back online or available then send. It does not always mean an email address is bad.

Congratulations, you've ascended to the fifth challenge—spam traps!

Fifth Challenge

Spam Traps

There are two categories of spam traps you should be aware of: pure spam traps and recycled spam traps. Pure spam traps are the worst for your sender reputation, making it extremely difficult for you to deliver email to an Inbox if you're caught sending to one. Why are they so bad? Because pure spam trap email addresses are set up with the sole purpose of identifying spammers. In other words, there's no conceivable reason any sender should have that email address...unless they got it in a sketchy way. Recycled spam

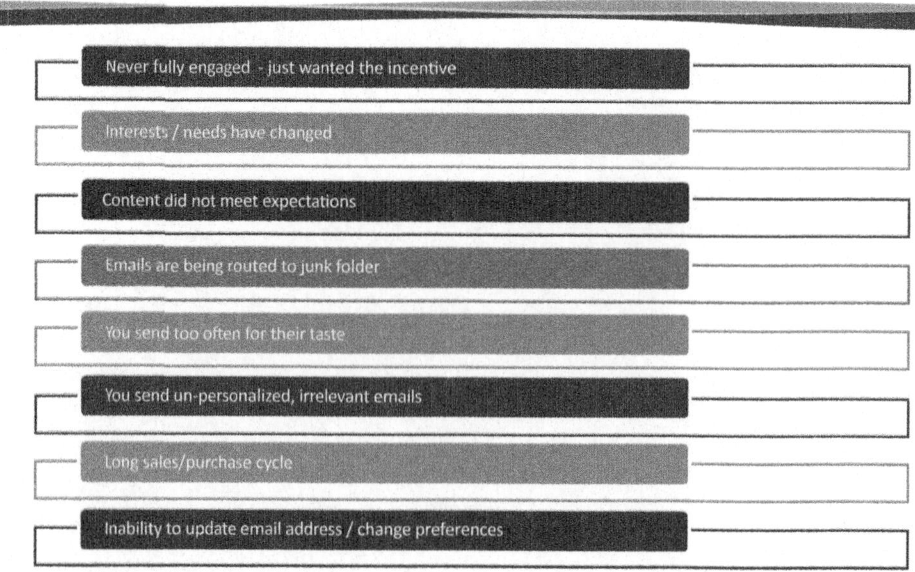

Why Recipients Go Inactive
Never fully engaged - just wanted the incentive
Interests / needs have changed
Content did not meet expectations
Emails are being routed to junk folder
You send too often for their taste
You send un-personalized, irrelevant emails
Long sales/purchase cycle
Inability to update email address / change preferences

Figure 7. Why Recipients Go Inactive (Source: Silverpop)

traps, on the other hand, could have been active email addresses at one point in time. That means they might have just gone dormant or inactive, and they've been taken over by the mailbox provider after a period of inactivity.

Could you have a spam trap on your list?

Maybe.

If you're sending to a purchased list, to an old portion of your list or to older, unengaged subscribers, it's possible you have a spam trap on your list that could impact your email deliverability.

By regularly monitoring your emails for complaints, hard bounces, and spam traps, you'll be protecting your reputation with mailbox providers and ensuring better email deliverability.

Beware of Three Traps

Typo Traps

Whether you're using misspelled domains, sending bulk emails, or sending emails to recipients that didn't intentionally subscribe (batch and blast), your email marketing efforts are being sent to spam.

Poor email list lead-gathering practices will produce a bad online reputation for your brand and could potentially lead you down the path of hitting spam traps.

Have you ever misspelled "Google" and it came out as "Gogle," but it still took you directly to Google.com? Or have you sent out an email to "Gmall" or "Comnast?" This where typo traps come from. They are real emails that will not bounce and have misspelled domains. Typo traps are the most common types of spam traps. Mailbox providers watch these spam traps to get an insight into senders' list practices. When sending an email, a best practice is to send a confirmation email and suppress that email address if they don't confirm. Typo traps are there to catch senders who don't confirm opt-ins and don't keep a clean list. Some networks will see this as evidence of abusive practices. To avoid a typo trap, clean your list and confirm opt-ins.

Grey or Recycled Trap

Remember your first email address? You probably don't use it anymore, right? Guess what, there is a high chance a mailbox provider has reactivated it to see what brands are still sending messages to it. This is called a grey or recycled trap. It's important to be in control of your lists from opt-ins to hard bounces or unsubscribes. Recycled traps don't turn into recycled traps until after they hard bounce, so when using a list from an affiliate, make sure to grab their suppression list as well. That way you can avoid sending to addresses that have already hard bounced. Remember, once an address is a spam trap, it doesn't hard bounce any more. Purchased lists are often riddled with old addresses that have become spam traps. To avoid recycled spam traps, permanently suppress hard bounces, segment out unengaged users, and don't use lists if you don't know they were collected with good opt-in practices.

Pristine Trap

The third spam trap is called a pristine spam trap. A pristine spam trap is an email address created by a mailbox provider or blacklist, and then used to register for forums and posted on blogs, etc., where list scrapers will see it. That list you purchased that you think is going to drive massive revenue was usually scraped off the Internet and is full of pristine spam traps. Mailbox providers and blacklists consider sending to users who don't expect your mail to be one of the most abusive practices. To protect their customers, these networks will filter and even block senders who hit pristine spam traps.

In conclusion, to avoid spam traps, set good expectations, use double opt-in, and segment out unengaged users. There is no way to definitively identify all spam traps already on your list, but if you are segmenting by engagement, they will be segmented out with the rest of the unengaged users.

Brands end up blacklisted, filtered, and blocked due to poor sending practices. Always keep a suppression list of emails that should not receive your messages and only send to engaged users who've requested to receive your emails.

By following these simple steps and best practices, you might find your email messages on the "nice list" with mailbox providers this year.

A More Sinister Trap

There has been an increase in smarter phishers. Logos now are crisp and clear and clean where they used to be pixelized. Addresses, links, footers are more effective because it looks more official until you look at the FROM email address. What I always say is if you hover over the link that says CLICK HERE, it will be a long line of gibberish that makes no sense. It's not taking you to PayPal or Bank of America. The emails look more legitimate than they used to. We've seen an uptick in hacking and downloading a zip file. If it was an email meant for junk folder, it's a false promise. On any given day, 90+ percent of all email traffic coming into Yahoo! is spam. Filters are changing and evolving all day. If you are trying to sell purple dinosaurs, there is spam coming in from China that uses the term, purple dinosaur, and you are trying to use that phrase legitimately, you will have a hard time reaching the Inbox.

These spam filters evolve thousands of times a day so what worked last week may not work this week just because someone may have stolen your brand or link. A lot of people complained that your brand didn't coincide with what you promised them because this spammer hijacked your message. It's about meeting my expectation upon signing up for your brand email. Marketers can see if a user unsubscribes, if you open it, but there is so much happening that the mailbox provider can only see.

If you are trying to manipulate Gmail by opening up 500 accounts, Gmail knows all these accounts are brand new and that you are accessing them from same location based on your IP address. Trying to game the system is not going to work.

If you are sending an email to Gmail, they have thousands of servers around the world and will take whatever email you throw in. The odds are good that they will accept it. But if you are sending to a small business domain with one server and sending to 100 people at that small business, you look like a spammer. That email server is much more likely than Gmail to limit or reject your emails.

Email Drunk and the Increase in Spam

Even when offering an outstanding webinar or white paper, which is valuable content, marketers sometimes "send it and forget it." They risk the campaign by not consistently tracking results. Clients come to us all the time and say, "Our email performed well last week at 20 percent open rate, and we sent the same email this week and it dropped to 3 percent open rate. What happened?" Filters change. Complaints change. Which negatively affected your domain? The content was great last week, but it has since been fingerprinted or filtered because of spam from China and Russia and overseas. Your domain has been phished. I hear too often that marketers don't have time. They don't test. In this space you can't have that. You need to constantly test and tweak, and stay ahead of the curve. Do you have authentication? Is your content this? Do you have a dedicated or shared IP? Tweaking subject lines, content, links, images. Testing to make sure image and link work. If something is broken, unsubscribes and complaints go up. They ask, "Are they trying to steal my identity?"

We live in a world where people are email drunk. We know if we give someone an email address, they're going to use it. When you sign up for a credit card, purchase something from the mall, we don't read terms and conditions or privacy policy. It's an acceptable form of communication. The problem comes when email is irrelevant or cadence and frequency is too much. If images and links are broken or alignment is off, is this really you? Sam's Club? Costco? Testing and render-ability can affect Inbox placement.

Say No to the No-Reply

Why would you not encourage your subscribers to interact with you and your brand? That is the feeling most recipients have when they receive an email from a brand with a "no-reply" email address. So, you want to send me promotional emails so I will purchase or convert, but you don't want to hear from me?!

Most mailbox providers will not allow the email recipient to add a no-reply email to your address book. If the recipient cannot add you to their address book, you could be more likely to be flagged as spam and sent to the junk folder. It is also much more likely for subscribers to hit the spam button if they can't reply back requesting removal of their email address.

You should also remember that if a recipient replies to the sender's email address, the mailbox provider might automatically add them as a safe sender. This is a huge benefit to the sender if they can get added to the recipient's whitelist. Safe sender privileges include bypassing some of the mailbox provider's mail filters and delivering to the recipient's Inbox.

Often, spam filters and the recipient's personal security settings are set up to send no-reply email addresses to the junk folder. This will decrease overall deliverability rates and possible conversions.

There has been a large upswing with recipients opening emails on their mobile device. Mobile devices don't just show the name of the sender; they show your email address as well. As a sender, would you open an email with a no-reply email address?

Some people will not click the unsubscribe link, but will reply to your email asking to be removed. The reason some of these email recipients will not click on the unsubscribe link is because they feel that doing so will flood their mailbox with more email. Make sure that you honor these requests and suppress the email addresses from your list. The last thing you want is for these recipients to click the spam button on future emails and hurt your IP and domain reputation.

Increased Message Acceptance

As much as I caution against hurting your domain reputation, I enthusiastically push advanced deliverability tools such as *seed list testing* and *panel data*. SparkPost explains both in the most straightforward way:

> A sender includes special 'seed' (test) email addresses at various ISPs among the recipients of their campaign. The seed list service providers then monitor those accounts with tools that determine where your email landed in their seed account—the inbox, the spam folder,… or perhaps if didn't arrive at all. Because seed lists employ a known (and relatively small) set of addresses to test, they can give an answer about email performance of a particular campaign to those specific addresses. However, the information learned from seed lists should be considered at best directional. They can't give you a comprehensive assessment of performance.

That's where one more way to measure deliverability performance really becomes important: panel data. While seed lists use definitive results for specific email messages at a small number of addresses to extrapolate overall campaign performance, panels take something of the reverse approach. Panel providers like eDataSource monitor millions of real-world recipient inboxes (the owners of said mailboxes have agreed to participate in the research, by the way!) and aggregate data about message characteristics and performance over time. Thus, while seed lists are good leading indicators of the efficacy of a particular campaign, panel data is best for assessing broad slices of real-world performance.

Voices of Deliverability Inferno

Brad Gurley, Sr. Director of Deliverability, Real Magnet

Which spam traps are the most harmful? Why? How do you monitor?

Pristine traps are most likely to cause delivery issues like blacklisting, but marketers who try to follow best practices are rarely going to see this type of trap. Recycled traps are dangerous particularly for organizations who do not regularly prompt members to reconfirm or update their details. Sending to old lists of members or customers—a fairly common practice—often causes this type of trap hit. For senders who collect addresses via point-of-sale entry, typo traps are especially problematic.

How will DMARC improve overall spam filtering?

DMARC will help block spam and phishing attempts from spoofed domains, but does nothing to stop properly authenticated domains from sending spam. In addition, the fact that so many legitimate senders use "cousin" domains for things like satisfaction surveys, etc. means that spammers can use the same tactics with a high level of success.

Can you share a horror story or lesson learned?

My Lesson: Double-check your bounce handling, then check it again regularly. Errors in asynchronous bounce handling aren't always easily spotted, so they can go on for months or years unchecked. I've seen such an error cause a major Spamhaus listing that took hundreds of hours of resources to resolve.

Congratulations, you've ascended to the sixth challenge—blacklists!

Sixth Challenge

Blacklists

If you know you're on a blacklist, how do you get off? Sorry to tell you, but you got on there because of complaints and/or spam trap hits. People often call us after being put on a blacklist. We are mediators between ISPs, mailbox providers, blacklists and email marketers. Marketers want to have blocks removed, to understand bounces and to find out why their reputation is dropping. All of that is critical to keep moving emails, but they need to know the reasons and learn how not to do it again.

You will have stronger email delivery if you can verify emails are not on these blacklists. SpamCop, SORBS, and Spamhaus are only three of many blacklist reporting services on the web. Many blacklists will block IP's and/or domains. It's important to understand email deliverability best practices while approaching blacklist related issues.

Spamhaus

The Spamhaus Project is an international organization, based in both London and Geneva, founded in 1998 to track email spammers and spam-related activity.

The purpose behind their organization is to create a "block" list of senders who have bad sending reputations. This list's senders have shown poor sending practices by sending spam to Spamhaus' partners or to their spam traps. Spamhaus will remember their IP and/or domain and publicly post them. Internet service providers and email servers use Spamhaus' block list to reduce the amount of spam that reaches their users. You will have stronger email delivery if you can verify emails are not on these blacklists.

An IP or domain that's put on Spamhaus has shown prolonged poor sending practices. During this time, its B-to-B and B-to-C deliverability will both be significantly diminished. It's used by Yahoo!, AOL, and Hotmail, as well as dozens of mailbox providers in around the world and uncountable corporate email servers. No other blacklist comes close to affecting this volume, making Spamhaus a top priority for monitoring and remediating.

Just to give you an example of the power that Spamhaus enforces, consider this tale from the trenches: A client had uploaded contacts to a platform like Eloqua. That company knew nothing about this purchased list and started using the list. No validation, no opt-in, no hygiene. Their IP got listed on Spamhaus, which is the worst blacklist to be on. Not only did Spamhaus list their marketing infrastructure IP addresses; they also listed their sending domain, landing page domains, corporate domain, mail server IP address...all Internet destinations tied to their entire organization. You could not get to that company's website, send and receive email within, or access landing pages. As a result, they were shut down!

Receiving that call for help was interesting, needless to say. We had to diagnose the problem and scrutinize that strange list that marketing had blindly used, which literally had shut them down. Sub-domains could not be created. IP space could not be purchased. Spamhaus wanted to draw a line in the sand. In turn, the company sought legal counsel in order to sue them for their losses. That was fruitless, as you may guess, because Spamhaus had every right to blacklist them.

We helped the company clean up their database and remove that bad list from their marketing efforts. We worked night and day for a week, mining data, communicating with Spamhaus and negotiating the terms that all parties would agree on. Some of the people on that list had actually clicked and purchased something from the company, but those new customers also had to be deleted.

Just keep in mind that when you want to grow your list as a good revenue source and to increase brand awareness, bulk lists almost never mean hygienic lists.

SORBS (Spam and Open-Relay Blocking System)

SORBS has a block list of over 12 million host servers known to disseminate spam, phishing attacks, and other forms of malicious email. Over 200,000 corporations worldwide use SORBS, making it a very significant concern for B-to-B senders.

SORBS uses partner spam reports and spam traps to identify and list IP addresses that show bad sending practices. A sender can also be put on SORBS from a recommendation by anyone. Fortunately, in an effort to reduce false positives (senders who are careless and not malicious), SORBS will remove offending IPs on request after 48 hours of no spam. However, repeat listings will lengthen the delisting time and SORBS will eventually stop delisting a repeat offender.

SORBS has a low false-positive rate, making it very popular and therefore a top priority for monitoring and remediation, especially for B-to-B senders.

SpamCop

SpamCop is an email spam reporting service. If you are sending unsolicited bulk or commercial email, your recipients have the option to report your IP address to SpamCop's analysis. This is where your IP address gets on SpamCop's blocklist. Therefore, an IP will be put on SpamCop from complaints of spam from that IP.

While filing spam reports, network administrators who use SpamCop will receive a list of IP addresses that are not allowed access into networks. So if you are sending email to a network that uses SpamCop from a computer whose IP is on their blocklist, your mail will be blocked and not deliver.

It takes upkeep to unblock your IP address from SpamCop. Mainly because they handle blocking and unblocking on their own. If SpamCop continues to receive reports of spam originating from the networks you are responsible for, those networks will continue to be listed. If you can keep up with deliverability best practices, then you will be delisted by SpamCop automatically after 24 hours.

SpamCop, SORBS, and Spamhaus are only three of many blacklist reporting services on the web. To prevent from getting your IP or domain listed on a blacklist, follow email deliverability best practices.

Keep a clean list while updating hygiene continuously, stay on top of bounce logs, and keep an eye on the content you are sending out. Spam filters are continuously changing, therefore it's good to have someone watching them, as it will prevent you from being blacklisted.

Feedback Loops

A feedback loop is a term that I often hear email marketers confuse with "email replies" and "email forwarding." A feedback loop is when the mailbox provider/network forwards complaints of your recipients to the organization that sent the email. Typically, this is sent back to the Email Service Provider that sent your emails. Not all mailbox providers and networks maintain a feedback loop, but it is important to get signed up with all that are available. If you use an Email Service Provider, they will typically take care of signing you up and processing these complaints so they will be suppressed from further email campaigns.

Feedback loops are a good metric and measurement to identify problems with your marketing campaigns. Again, not all mailbox providers and domains that you send to have the ability to send back those people who mark the emails as "Junk" or "Spam." Always review your campaign reports for "complaints" and research the trends that go along with your marketing programs. Some complaints are a positive sign too. Your recipients cannot complain if the email lands in the junk folder, so complaints can show positive Inbox placement. Constantly ask yourself:

∞ Did complaints go up because your subscribers did not find your content relevant?

∞ Did a certain piece of content or subject line generate a larger number of complaints?

∞ Did the older, inactive list spike your complaints?

∞ Is your unsubscribe link broken?

New feedback loops come out frequently and it is always a good idea to check and see if you are signed up for any new ones. The one major mailbox provider that does not have a traditional feedback loop is Gmail. Gmail does offer your ESP the ability to receive alerts based upon complaints they are seeing on your marketing campaigns. Below are the ones that are currently available as of this book's release:

∞ AOL

∞ Blue Tie

∞ Comcast

∞ Cox

∞ EarthLink

∞ FastMail

∞ ItaliaOnLine

∞ La Poste

∞ Mail.ru

∞ Microsoft

∞ Rackspace

∞ Synacor

∞ Telenor

∞ Tucows (OpenSRS)

∞ United Online

∞ USA.net

∞ Yahoo!

∞ XS4ALL

∞ Yandex

∞ Zoho

Congratulations, you've ascended to the seventh challenge—authentication!

Seventh Challenge

Authentication

Now you know that a large part of email deliverability comes down to taking every step possible to avoid being perceived as a spammer in the eyes of spam filters and your recipients.

One of the most definitive ways in which you can affect this is by authenticating your emails. Authentication allows mailbox providers to acknowledge the legitimacy of your email sends.

So, what is email authentication?

Authentication is a way to prove an email is not forged. Authentication technology gives the recipient mail servers a record of identification to check, to ensure the sender is legitimate. Emails that fail to pass authentication checks may be blocked or put through additional filters, potentially preventing them from reaching the Inbox.

Email services like AOL, Gmail or Yahoo! (as well as corporate email servers) use one or more of these authentication methods to verify sender identity: DKIM (Domain Keys Identified Mail) and SPF (Sender Policy Framework).

Why is Authentication Important?

Many email providers use authentication, among other things, to track sender reputation. Without it, the chances of your emails being filtered are much higher.

Email authentication allows mailbox providers to properly identify the sender of the email so they can make smarter decisions about the

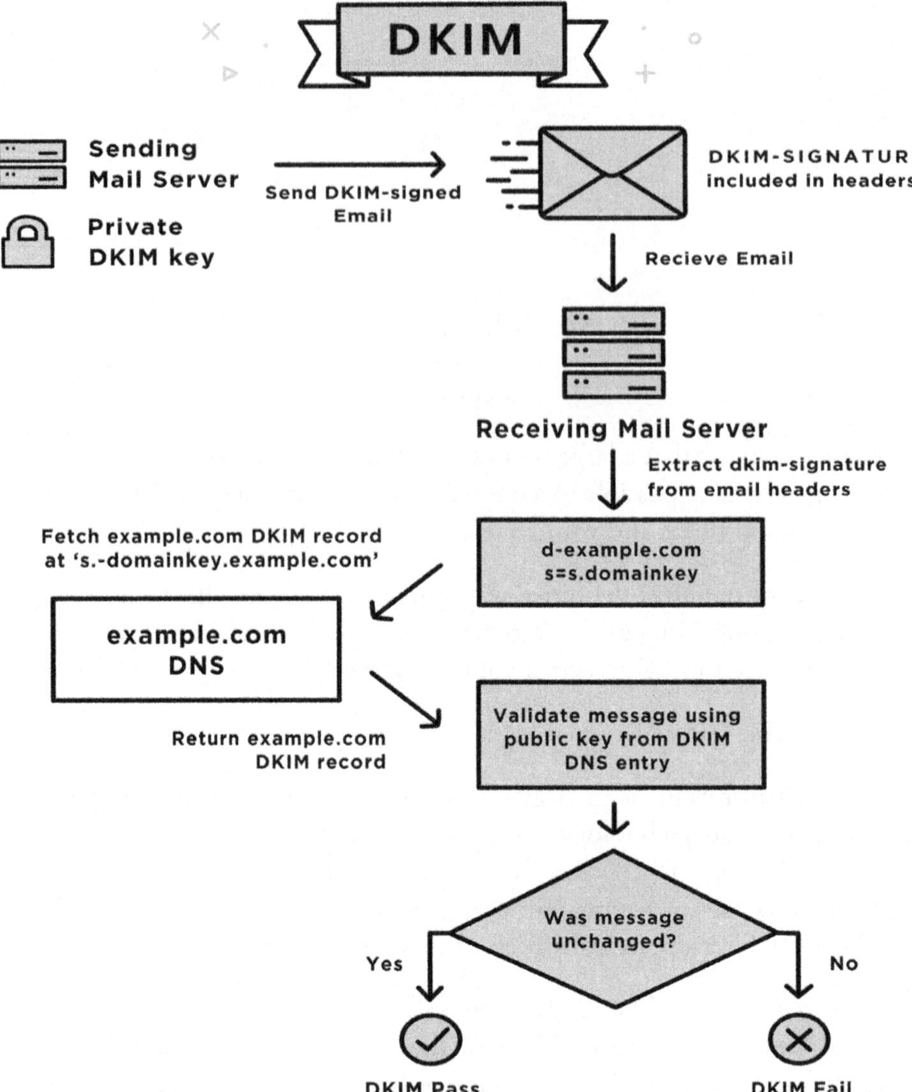

Figure 8. How DKIM Works (Source: Postmark)

delivery of your mail. Authentication has become a best practice for email senders since spammers have gotten really smart about disguising malicious email under the veil of a trusted brand.

In today's world, email authentication is important for legitimate organizations in order to secure their online reputation and maintain customer trust in their brand. And anything that can impact email deliverability in a positive or negative way certainly demands your attention.

Authentication can be tricky, but take the time to check with your ESP and make sure the email you are sending is authenticated with both SPF and DKIM.

DKIM is essentially a public/private key cryptography pair. ESPs and mail servers will hold the private key but they give you the public key to update on your DNS. What happens is when I send an email, I send that information to the mailbox provider. They look up the public key and use the private key to match and authenticate.

Google's DKIM key was hacked a few years ago so they've made changes in the encryption levels. The problem is, it does not protect your brand from phishing and spoofing. It passes or fails. Bank of America, PayPal, eBay were getting phished and SPF and DKIM do not help with that. DMARC does. If you add a DMARC DNS entry on your domain, certain mailbox providers will send you reports that say here are all the IP addresses using your domain to send out email. You can see that someone in Russia is using your domain to send out 100,000 emails a day. You go through a data provider and then there are tools, which suck in all those files and show it on a dashboard to say, here is volume by day, country, sender.

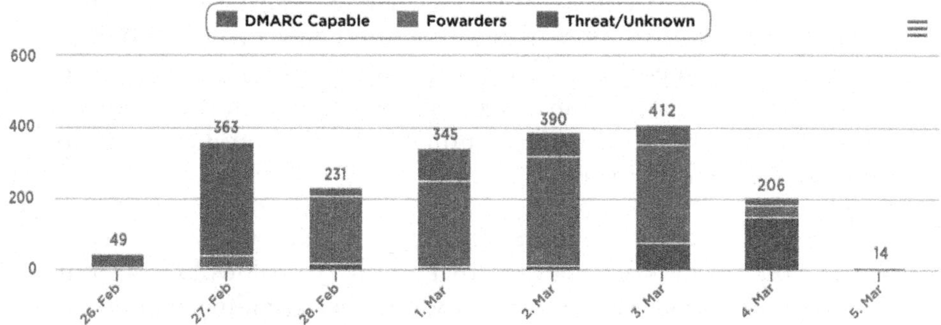

Figure 9. Sample DMARC Dashboard (Source: dmarcian)

With DMARC, there are three switches. *None* means don't do anything with my mail but tell me if somebody is using my domain to send out emails. I'm getting reports but not affecting the mail stream. Next is *quarantine*, which means if it does not come from the location I've specified in my DNS record, send it straight to the junk folder. The third option is *reject*: If it does not come from me, bounce it.

The problem is for major enterprise senders, who have multiple systems to send out email—payroll, HR, transactional, customer support—how do you combat that? You create subdomains for each one of those groups. That way, nobody else will use that domain to send the email. If they do, they're impersonating you as a brand. Brand and identity protection are critical to deliverability because if someone is using your domain to send out phishing emails, what will happen to the real messages coming from your domain?

DMARC is a great tool that allows the user to see what emails are being sent to twenty monitored domains on a daily basis. Scroll down and see things like sources, noncompliant sources, people forwarding their mail, and threats. I can see 1.7 million over the course of the week. You see the volume and get a baseline and understanding of legitimate sources or if someone is trying to phish or spoof you. You see compliance across the board. You understand your brand more fully. With threats, you see unidentified sources that can be problematic, aiming to phish you or spoof you. The result: 1711 messages spread over three mailbox providers, not passing SPF, not passing DKIM, not passing DMARC. They could be one-offs, but we can start to identify from domain and IP and start locking it down. All these IP addresses from China and Russia are sending out small messages, but they're failing at everything. This takes it to the next level, a newer form of identification. Now that you've identified it, put a strategy together. First, catalog all of the systems using your domain to send emails. Then create subdomains and progressively lock the DMARC record down from None to Quarantine to Reject. You don't want to implement Reject off the bat.

The truth is that though most fraud is perpetuated by an outside source, you can monitor your internal activity with DMARC also. It shows any other email service provider source that is sending mail within your organization. A large client had three email service providers—so they thought. We turned on DMARC to see all the sending sources, which turned out to be *eighteen*. This is a great example of sales and marketing personnel being in conflict. Sales did not want to go to marketing or other parts of their organization to request additional email campaigns. They wanted to send the messages on their own, so they signed up for free accounts everywhere and then Constant Contact, which could be costly. In essence, these rogue salespeople paid out of pocket just to send to bad lead lists. The problem is that Sales and Marketing teams both affect each other. With DMARC, we could easily show the organization that Salesforce and Eloqua were only two vendors of eighteen because sales people were using it to send out their own mail (which was not likely branded correctly either).

Going rogue to try to meet quotas is a common internal problem in a lot of Fortune 500 companies, which do not have DMARC turned on, and if they do, they're not reading the reports. Many of these reports go to a black hole.

Using DMARC, you can receive reports, put them in a dashboard and glean the suspects. It's like identifying fingerprints with a swab.

Prevention of Sin and Shame

Gmail offers a reputation tool, Gmail.com/Postmaster which provides insight into IP reputation, domain reputation, authentication, delivery errors. It is data right from the source and it's free. Sign up and Gmail sends you information, a dashboard and a graph that shows what they think of you. Microsoft Outlook has something similar. Microsoft SNDS, Smart Network Data Services, allows you to see what Outlook thinks of you. This information is gold. It helps us do our job and understand at what point, at what area did your IP or domain name tank. AOL has their own. Put your IP address in and it shows if you are good, bad or neutral. Third-party tools will check your reputation. They gather data on their own and give you a score. I always tell marketers to not focus on one particular area of data, but look at everything across the board. People will score you differently based on what they receive. Gmail has no idea what you are doing with Outlook. You may be having problems you don't know about.

How do you want people to see you? With your brand, step out with your best foot forward to meet the community and show that you are a good sender and not sending to people that complain or don't exist.

Congratulations, you've ascended to the eighth challenge—compliance! Keep going, you're so close to Paradise!

Eighth Challenge

Compliance

Recently, a major brand said, "Help us, Gmail hates us!" The problem was all their emails were going into the Promotions folder. They wanted to be in the Primary folder and got a lot of open rates because people were curious. Being creative helps.

We review content including every HTML link to see where it goes. We look at the reputation of those links. If you have affiliates or third-party ads, be careful about where that link in your branded ad goes. Know your partners, your affiliates. They are responsible for whatever is in that ad. A lot of people don't take time to test or think it is a priority. It could affect Inbox placement for the primary brand though because other shady things are embedded in that ad. It happens all the time, especially on the B-to-B side. B-to-B marketers buy lists and leads.

How can I maximize my buying? Send a bunch of leads. Think of Google Ads. Some spend their email marketing budget on Google Ads. Google Ads can get out of control quickly. The price differs based on other people that are bidding for that word. Certain words would be $100 or $500 a click based on a key word. Google Ad Words has a place in a marketing strategy which should include email and social. They all play their parts. It's a matter of where you want to place your dollars to achieve the best ROI.

Everyone says email has the highest amount of ROI based on what you're paying for. I can reach two people on Google Ads and they may never convert. It's a risk. It is a great way to attract individuals and demonstrate brand identity, but it's a mistake to rely only on it.

People are using email for not just information you're receiving but as a to-do list, extensions for your calendar, contacts. Depending on how far you go back, email can be used for record-keeping, documentation of a process or conversation. Google and Google search and integration with Gmail, which includes your Inbox, is thorough. That said, I try to operate at Inbox Zero every day not only for minimalist purposes but also, to adhere to compliance.

Any email in my Inbox is my to-do list. My wife, on the other hand, has thousands of emails in her Inbox. In Gmail, she will star them to make sure important brands to her make it into her Inbox. Email is different for everyone. When I worked at a law firm, they used Microsoft Outlook and I would talk from a legal perspective: create subfolders, save emails accordingly, but you must organize them. Having any sort of number ticking off of an app on the phone anywhere bothers me.

But I don't create laws!

Keep Laws and Regulations at the Forefront of Your Sending Patterns

CAN-SPAM

As senders, we must understand CAN-SPAM (Controlling the Assault of Non-Solicited Pornography And Marketing Act) and the repercussions that could ensue if not followed. Deliverability and reputation are important, but if you're not following the rules (laws and regulations) then you may find yourself in more hot water than just an IP/domain that has a bad reputation.

CAN-SPAM is what is known as an "opt-out" law, meaning that every email is required to provide an obvious way for the recipient to choose to never be contacted again. This can be offered via unsubscribe link, preference page, or email address, but it must not require undue effort, and is recommended to only take one click to avoid spam complaints. While it is allowed for the sender to continue to send for 10 business days after an unsubscribe request, this is strongly not recommended as it will lead to a high volume of spam complaints. Additionally, CAN-SPAM requires that emails be upfront about their nature, that is, it is unlawful to disguise a marketing email with a correspondence-style subject line. While CAN-SPAM does not provide for a private right of action, meaning only the FCC may pursue a perpetrator, and therefore suits are rare, they have stiff penalties and the mailbox providers enforce the provisions themselves through filtering and by blocking offenders, whether the sender is caught by the FCC or not.

CAN-SPAM covers all commercial messages in the United States, which the law defines as "any electronic mail message the primary purpose of which is the commercial advertisement or promotion of a commercial product or service," including email that promotes content on commercial websites. The law makes no exception for business-to-business email.

Each separate email in violation of the CAN-SPAM Act is subject to penalties of up to $16,000.

Requirements under the Federal Trade Commission are:

1. *Don't use false or misleading header information.* Your "From," "To," "Reply-To," and routing information—including the originating domain name and email address—must be accurate and identify the person or business who initiated the message.

2. *Don't use deceptive subject lines.* The subject line must accurately reflect the content of the message.

3. *Identify the message as an ad.* The law gives you a lot of leeway in how to do this, but you must disclose clearly and conspicuously that your message is an advertisement.

4. *Tell recipients where you're located.* Your message must include your valid physical postal address. This can be your current street address, a post office box you've registered with the U.S. Postal Service, or a private mailbox you've registered with a commercial mail receiving agency established under Postal Service regulations.

5. *Tell recipients how to opt out of receiving future email from you.* Your message must include a clear and conspicuous explanation of how the recipient can opt out of getting email from you in the future. Craft the notice in a way that's easy for an ordinary

person to recognize, read, and understand. Creative use of type size, color, and location can improve clarity. Give a return email address or another easy Internet-based way to allow people to communicate their choice to you. You may create a menu to allow a recipient to opt out of certain types of messages, but you must include the option to stop all commercial messages from you. Make sure your spam filter doesn't block these opt-out requests.

6. *Honor opt-out requests promptly.* Any opt-out mechanism you offer must be able to process opt-out requests for at least 30 days after you send your message. You must honor a recipient's opt-out request within 10 business days. You can't charge a fee, require the recipient to give you any personally identifying information beyond an email address, or make the recipient take any step other than sending a reply email or visiting a single page on an Internet website as a condition for honoring an opt-out request. Once people have told you they don't want to receive more messages from you, you can't sell or transfer their email addresses, even in the form of a mailing list. The only exception is that you may transfer the addresses to a company you've hired to help you comply with the CAN-SPAM Act.

7. *Monitor what others are doing on your behalf.* The law makes clear that even if you hire another company to handle your email marketing, you can't contract away your legal responsibility to comply with the law. Both the company whose product is promoted in the message and the company that actually sends the message may be held legally responsible.

CASL

Anyone sending email TO a recipient accessing emails in Canada or sending email FROM Canada is covered by CASL (Canada Anti-Spam Law). If your organization is located in the US, EU, or anywhere in the world and sends Commercial Electronic Messages (CEM) to Canada, you are still responsible for complying with CASL.

The price of non-compliance? Of course there is one! And it's hefty.

For organizations, violations of CASL may result in payment of an administrative monetary penalty (AMP) up to $10 million per violation. Directors, officers, agents and mandataries of a corporation may face individual liability under CASL and be subject to an AMP up to $1 million per violation.

Under the Canadian Radio-television and Telecommunications Commission, there are three general requirements for sending the CEM to an electronic address: (1) consent, (2) identification information and (3) an unsubscribe mechanism.

Consent

All senders must obtain either *express* or *implied* consent before sending commercial electronic messages to individuals. The onus is on the sender to prove they have obtained consent to send a message. Sender should document when consent was obtained, why consent was obtained, and the manner in which it was obtained at minimum. When obtaining consent, it needs to be clear to recipients that even if they give consent now, they can revoke it in the future.

Identification

Each CEM must identify the sender of the message and contact information. A mailing address consists of the sender's valid, current street (or civic) address, postal box address, rural route address, or general delivery address. In addition, a phone number and/or website address must be included.

Unsubscribe

Unsubscribe mechanisms must be included in a CEM and must be set out clearly and prominently. The unsubscribe must be readily performed, accessed without difficulty or delay and should be simple, quick and easy for consumers to use. Any unsubscribe requests must be honored immediately or within 10 days. The unsubscribe must be valid for a minimum of 60 days after the message has been sent.

Similarities and Differences Between CAN-SPAM and CASL

The main difference between these laws is that CAN-SPAM is an opt-out law whereas CASL is an opt-in law. CASL is the strictest global anti-spam law. In order to email a recipient, you must have consent through an opt-in mechanism where the recipient must take an action to give that consent. For example, provide a check in a checkbox; acknowledge with an action that he/she would like to receive future messages. Under CAN-SPAM, you are able to email without prior consent; however, you must honor the opt-out promptly.

GDPR

Now, on to a forthcoming law that will affect companies operating in the European Union: General Data Protection Regulation (GDPR), circa May 25, 2018. This law will be one law that will be a uniform regulation across all EU member states, resolving the lack of harmonization across the EU. GDPR will supersede national laws, although local laws apply in some instances. The GDPR applies to processing carried out by organizations operating within the EU. It also applies to organizations outside the EU that offer goods or services to individuals in the EU.

Key terms include:

∞ *Personal Data*—Any information relating to an identified or identifiable natural person ("data subject"); an identifiable person is one who can be identified, directly or indirectly, in particular by reference to an identifier such as a name, an identification number, location data, online identifier or to one or more factors specific to the physical, physiological, genetic, mental, economic, cultural or social identity of that person.

∞ *Sensitive Personal Data*—Personal data, revealing racial or ethnic origin, political opinions, religious or philosophical beliefs, trade-union membership; data concerning health or sex life and sexual orientation; genetic data or biometric data.

∞ *Processor*—A natural or legal person, public authority, agency or any other body which processes personal data on behalf of the controller.

∞ *Controller*—The natural or legal person, public authority, agency or any other body which alone or jointly with others determines the purposes and means of the processing of personal data; where the purposes and means of processing are determined by EU or Member State laws, the controller (or the criteria for nominating the controller) may be designated by those laws.

What will it cost you to break the GDPR law once it is established? Fines up to 20 million Euro or up to 4 percent of total annual worldwide revenue, whichever is higher.

Compliance Can Get You to Paradise

Per the above, it is critical that you have the following to remain in compliance with these laws:

- Ensure you have opt-in permission for all messages sent. This means that a user takes action to request or accept future messages from sender.
- Good record-keeping is critical. For every recipient in your list, ensure you are keeping an audit trail of permission including where, when and how the recipient provided consent. The onus is on the sender to ensure that demonstrating sufficient permission can be upheld in court.
- All messages must be properly identified and use the prescribed information on each electronic message sent and/or sign up page.
- Under CASL, pre-checked boxes are not considered affirmative consent.

If you need more inspiration to follow the laws, consider two companies that did not, according to the CRTC.

Compu-Finder, $1.1 million penalty

Violated basic principles of the law by continuing to send unsolicited commercial electronic messages after the law came into force to email addresses it found by scouring websites.

Plenty of Fish, $48,000 penalty

Complaints alleging that the company sent emails regarding PlentyofFish.com services to registered users that did not include a clear and prominent unsubscribe mechanism that could be readily performed.

Is Your Reputation Impacting Your Email Deliverability?

Your reputation matters. As a business owner, you know that your reputation is important and when it comes to email deliverability, your reputation as an email sender matters. The better your email reputation, the more emails make it to the Inboxes of your recipients.

The first step is determining your email reputation. Is your email reputation affecting your email deliverability? Your email reputation is the measurement of the quality of your list and the extent that you follow best email practices. To find out what mailbox providers and other email receivers think of your email-marketing program, there are multiple sites to review (included at the end of the book). You will receive a scoring metric and with this score, you'll know whether you need to continue following best email practices to protect your high score, or take action to improve your reputation.

One of the primary ways to build a strong email reputation is to send messages to users who have requested them. The best way to do that is by allowing users the opportunity to subscribe to email lists.

Because spammers often pretend they're someone they're not, ESPs take steps to ensure senders are accurately representing themselves. Senders should use all common forms of authentication to ensure they've covered their bases with ESPs by joining key verification registries, including: Sender Policy Framework (SPF), DomainKeys Identified Mail (DKIM), and Domain-based Message Authentication, Reporting and Conformance (DMARC).

One of the best ways to maintain email reputation is to keep an eye on engagement by monitoring bounce-backs, complaints, open rates and click-throughs. Test and refine constantly.

And it is worth repeating over and over again, provide eye-catching content and subject lines!

Mailbox providers also monitor recipient engagement, so senders should take steps to ensure their emails are attracting the attention of recipients. A few tips include: avoid HTML-only content, spell check, limit links, avoid URL shorteners, and most importantly provide great, relevant content.

Congratulations, you've ascended to the last (and loaded) challenge—technology!

Ninth Challenge

Technology

Tactics in marketing strategy in this era are abundant, but they must serve your company's needs as they pertain to your email campaign volume. The following information cannot be skirted just because creative development is sexier. You need the right platform, mail server and distribution channel so contacts see all that sexiness.

Mail Servers

A mail server is a dedicated computer with a static IP address that your mail client (Gmail, Outlook, Thunderbird, Apple Mail) talks to via SMTP and either POP3 or IMAP, and which uses a special program to route, receive, and store messages. That's all simple enough, but not exactly what you want to know.

To understand what makes a mail server special, let's break the parts down:

A physical server

The server should be a computer with sufficient processing power on a robust network switch, with a high-bandwidth Internet connection and a static IP address.

An MTA

The MTA, or mail transfer agent, is the program that turns your words into something ready to travel the Internet. It accepts messages from your mail client (aka mail user agent or MUA: Gmail, Outlook,

Thunderbird, Apple Mail, etc.) and uses SMTP (Simple Mail Transfer Protocol) to push them to their destination MTA where the MDA (mail delivery agent) uses POP3 (Post Office Protocol version 3) or IMAP (Internet Message Access Protocol) to place the message in the recipient's MUA (you might remember POP3 and IMAP from setting up your phone).

The MTA might sound simple in theory, but there's a lot going on behind the scenes to make everything happen smoothly across millions upon millions of machines.

To start with, an MTA handles your domain. A domain is a type of address that lives in the DNS. When you look up an email domain in the DNS, it points to the location of an MTA that is set up to consider what domain is the "local" domain. In other words, if your MTA serves its own domain and if it receives an email addressed to any other domain, it looks up that domain in the DNS and passes the message along. Of course, if it receives an email addressed to its local domain, it keeps the email.

Including the host in the address is called "qualification" and if the receiving MTA is not set up with the correct qualification for the addressee, nothing gets delivered and the email bounces.

This means that the MTA needs to have recorded what host information (internal address) to give to each user at its domain (external address). Now, it makes sense that the MTA can't have two identical users even if they are on different domains. Once the email enters the correct MTA, the external address (domain) no longer matters and doesn't make the users unique anymore, meaning their hosts (internal addresses) could end up identical and conflict. This is what a virtual domain solves: it makes the host addresses of users in the virtual domain unique from the other local domain, so there is no possible user address conflict and mail goes to the correct mailbox.

When an MTA sends an email to another MTA, it includes a reply-to and an envelope-from, which are not necessarily the same, but usually neither contain any host information at all—that info doesn't leave the mail server. This is because a fully qualified address is often long and complex and is also a useful thing for a bad actor to have, so an MTA does what's called "masquerading" and hides all of that detailed address information by pretending the mailbox lives at the domain before the message hits the Internet. This is why you just see domain and subdomain in your "To:" and "From:" fields.Now that the MTA knows the host information, the address is more specific, but how does it become a cheerful "bing" in my pocket? The answer is POP3 and IMAP. These are the same special connections that mail clients use to send mail to your server and the MDA (mail delivery agent) of the MTA uses them to find logged-in users and drops the messages into their MUAs (mail clients).

Especially for the consumer, most people use Gmail or Yahoo!. Most don't use a platform like Thunderbird or Apple Mail unless they want to offline or download messages. Most people want to keep their emails. For the B-to-B audience, Outlook is primarily used, while Google Apps and Office 365 hosting is becoming more prevalent. Hostingfacts.com notes that 64 percent of all business domains are now being hosted with Office 365 or Google Apps, which is astounding. People pay per mailbox per month to essentially offload that responsibility to Google or Microsoft. People still use Outlook to download their mail. You're downloading it off the server to free up valuable email space. Your mail client may restrict you and only give you 5 gigs of storage. You have to download it and archive it locally. That is one of the reasons people still use this platform.

Secondly, I would say mobile has taken over our lives. Cell phones, tablets. There is no need for some of these applications. You use the mail client on your phone. You use the Gmail app on your phone. That is kind of a change. Growing up, even in grad school, my first job required that we use Outlook; it had to be Outlook and have my folder structure. Mobile now makes everything easy. On your phone you've got your entire life. You can filter your folder, look at your calendar, see your contacts, interact with brands, reply, forward, star, save, and tag.

The shift in thinking to mobile has really changed the way people think about mail clients like Outlook. Another recent shift which was initially painful for marketers was the introduction by Gmail of a tabbed email or folder structure. Outlook has a similar concept called Focused Inbox. Gmail began sorting email into Primary, Update, Social and Promotion tabs based on their own classifications and algorithms. Users were just reading the Primary folder. That has been a shift. There are a lot of changes based upon user preference. I always tell people that Gmail is responsible for their users' mailboxes, both in privacy and security. They don't care where the email lands.

But you care. And you can make the Inbox, no matter the server behind it.

How to Get Emails Delivered to Microsoft

Emails delivered to Microsoft and AOL means you are following email deliverability best practices. Deliverability to Outlook.com is based on your reputation. Microsoft releases reputation data via its Smart Network Data Service (SNDS) program. Windows Live uses SPF and DKIM authentication. They filter email using Symantec/Brightmail Probe Network, SmartScreen filtering, and other content-level filtering. Blocking may result from being listed with Brightmail; removing those blocks requires contacting Symantec. The Outlook.com Smart Network Data Service (SNDS) gives you the data you need to understand and improve your reputation at Microsoft. Data includes filtering, complaint rate, and spam trap hits.

How to Get Emails Delivered to AOL

AOL focuses heavily on DKIM authentication and references the block lists maintained at The Spamhaus Project. Their spam filter is proprietary and custom-built. Metrics such as complaints, unknown users, content, bounce processing, and spam traps influence AOL's Inbox placement. If you need to view your reputation, find detailed bounce information, or open a ticket with the postmaster, AOL offers a postmaster site.

How to Get Email Delivered to Yahoo!

Want to scream, "Yahoo?" The key mission of Yahoo! is to deliver messages that people want to receive and filter messages they don't. With Yahoo!, you'll need to perform list management tasks frequently and monitor hard and soft bounces as well as inactive subscribers.

Sending email to users who aren't reading them or who mark them as "spam," will hurt your delivery metrics and reputation. Send email only to those who want it. Use an opt-in method of subscription for your mailing list and make sure subscribers have verified their intent to receive your mailings.

Review email content for common characteristics of spam. Test your emails' visual look with image placeholders. Many of your recipients won't see images in your email. Email on Acid is an excellent place you can go to check your message rendering.

Make sure you are linking to domains, not IP addresses. Yahoo! will filter out these links. Don't include HTML forms, JavaScript, or embedded objects (like Flash or ActiveX). Yahoo! will count these objects/forms against your reputation.

Have separate IPs depending on your mail stream (transactional, marketing, bulk, etc. Shared email services can have multiple domains using one IP to send email. If the same IPs are sending unsolicited commercial email and your reputation goes down, Yahoo! will hop on the wagon and filter your messages from that IP.

If your servers act as "open proxies" or "open relays," spammers may attempt to send their own mail from your systems. At a minimum, your SMTP servers should identify the originating IP addresses from the email and mention this in the email headers to help you diagnose spam problems.

Use bulk mail authentication best practices and review SMTP reply codes often. If your messages are being blocked, look closely at any SMTP error codes your mail servers are returning. Make sure you're addressing the root of the problem.

Here are proven bulk mail best practices:

∞ Don't retry 5xx messages. Retrying permanent errors increases the chances your mail will be de-prioritized.

∞ Retry 4xx messages. This is a temporary error.

∞ Enroll in the feedback loop if you're signing your emails with DKIM or DomainKeys. A feedback loop analysis can help you track and manage your spam complaint rates. Always make sure your emails include DKIM authenticated signatures. Check if you're DKIM signing the email. DKIM signature helps Yahoo! authenticate that email is safe, secure and from the senders who claim to send it. Not being DKIM signed makes your emails appear to be sent by a spammer.

∞ Publish reverse DNS (PTR) records for your sending IPs.

Yahoo! is more likely to downgrade an IP's sending reputation if there's no reverse DNS entry for your IP address or your mailing IP looks like a dynamically-assigned IP instead of a static mail server.

∞ Be CAN-SPAM and DMARC compliant. Invalid DMARC records can cause problems if you're sending from non-compliant bulk mailing services.

How to Get Email Delivered to Gmail

Filters are key to Gmail gold. Do an email deliverability test while sending out an email and see how many are being delivered to Gmail. This is the first step.

I'm sure you're wondering what Gmail looks for when processing Inbox placement, right? One is double opt-in/confirmed opt-in history. This is when someone signs up for emails and then has to verify that their information is correct. Therefore, it's a great idea to have an "add to address book" section or any confirming CTA that a recipient will click on in the first email. This button helps you pass spam filters a lot faster because it is similar to a personal whitelist for the user.

Use a list-unsubscribe link in the header. Gmail also looks for DKIM authentication and is leading the charge for DMARC with Microsoft. Gmail has a postmaster tools website (www.gmail.com/postmaster) where you can view the reputation of your IPs and Domains.

Secret tip: Gmail's classifier (spam filter) checks the WHOIS for domain registration. If it's hidden, it destroys your trust level.

Companies in Paradise

Not so fast! You're almost there, but before you ascend to Paradise, let's blaze through a review.

Subject line is key, along with your "from" name, which should remain consistent. That from name should align to what your buyers expect from that email. Sometimes for B-to-B and B-to-C, it's different. Catch someone's attention to get the coupon in the B-to-C, a shorter subject line. On B-to-B, it could be coming from an individual person, so if you always deal with Brian Smith, you know it will be from your Dell account representative or whatever. More of a one-to-one relationship. Those subject lines will also be longer. Certain details will make you open that if you're a B-to-B buyer. Know your audience.

Personas are great, but they can be demystified especially as they relate to different types of buyers. If I'm in IT and buying networking equipment, often I get bucketed in this list that likes text messages only. I don't read email in certain hours. I don't like wine and cars. Sometimes this information is really off and turns off a buyer. Get me to open the email. Millennials have less than two-second attention span. Once you have the email, grab their attention above that rectangle. What are you trying to sell me? Are there any links and images? What calls to actions? All this needs to be above the fold. It needs to grab my attention immediately so I can save, buy, forward. They know what you are doing with these emails. Brands and marketers have to understand that if email goes to Inbox or junk folder, things are happening in the background to get it there.

People forget things like preferences. Don't just opt me in, opt me down, change my frequency and cadence. The No. 1 reason people are complaining now is they are receiving too much email. You told me I would get one email and now I'm getting twenty, or I can't unsubscribe. I didn't sign up for your emails. This could land you on a blacklist or get your email shut down.

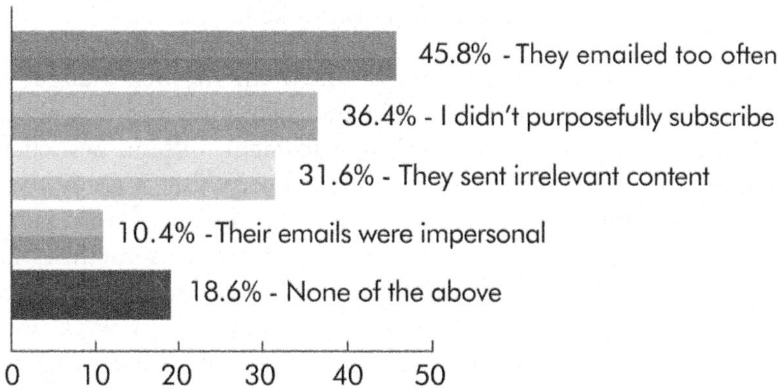

N=472 Source : TechnologyAdvice

Despite very specific preferences, headers can be the tipping point toward an open. The header includes things like time stamps on when sent or delivered, subject line, to, from, reply and authentication.

Did it pass SPF and DKIM? Does it have DMARC? The header also contains things like envelope-from address, which identifies or shows where bounces get sent back to. If an email bounced, where did it go? Filters will look at that envelope-from address and use it to categorize and establish a reputation for that domain. That is why when we work with clients, we look at the header specifically. Does all info match? We often find that they've got a custom subdomain, have their DKIM set up, but their envelope-from address is a shared domain. Because they didn't pay for branding or customization, it could have been an oversight. If it is shared, that means it's sharing reputation for other people using that. Dedicated IP or shared IP? If you are on shared, you could be on a shared pool with other people that have bad practices, bad lists, bad content. This could be bringing you down and you don't know it. You could be on a dedicated IP and you have bad practices or maybe you aren't adhering to certain volume standards.

If I am a brand name and sending 10,000 emails a month, I'll never get on a dedicated IP until I reach a sufficient volume. I've seen clients on the B-to-B side sending minimum 100,000 emails a month on a dedicated IP. On B-to-C, I'm seeing about 500,000 emails a month. The volume has to be there before you can establish your reputation. If you are on a dedicated IP and sending 5,000 or 10,000 a month, you're doing yourself more harm than good. Brands and marketers just want to start sending email. So much gets overlooked.

Marketers don't typically have a line item in their budget for deliverability. It should be included in their planning and they should take this seriously. It does mean Inbox placement. Oftentimes, clients will come to us when something is on fire. Everything is going to the junk folder in Gmail, AOL has blocked us, a number of reasons they come to us as an emergency. People do approach us sometimes and say they want to see how they're doing. Click rates may have been dropping. We'll do an audit. We can also monitor every week, every month. Some clients want to expand internationally so we work with them on that.

Email Deliverability Checklist

There's only one way your marketing emails can be opened, and that's if it's actually received by your subscribers. I have put together an email deliverability checklist to help you maximize email deliverability.

Send welcome emails.

Make a great first impression with customers and new email subscribers, by sending a welcome email. Using this first interaction as a starting block for brand recognition in their Inbox is a great way to build a list of active subscribers who will look forward to your emails.

Begin a reactivation campaign.

For anyone who last clicked or opened an email from you more than six months ago, send a new permission message so they can reconfirm that they'd like to be on your list. Eliminate all addresses that are unresponsive.

Clean up your email list.

Clean your email list at regular intervals for best results. Send out engagement mails to the recipients—remove the non-respondents—now you will have a list that is populated by interested people who are willing to engage with you. Targeting these respondents with your offers will help drive growth.

Minimize spam complaints.

Nothing tanks an IP reputation faster than spam complaints. It's a no-brainer (but good reminder) that you should only email individuals who have opted in to your campaigns.

Ramp up email volume cautiously.

Sudden volume fluctuations are red flags for many mailbox providers. Start by sending out small batches of emails that you know are engaged addresses to build trust in your IP with your Email Service Provider (ESP).

Use personalization and relevant content.

Standing out in Inboxes and making sure your content is relevant once your subscribers read it is paramount. And remember, subscribers who feel overwhelmed by irrelevant offers could be quick to flag your messages.

Monitor your results.

If you run into an issue with deliverability, you'll want to resolve it as swiftly as possible to help your emails reach the Inbox. Furthermore, by reviewing your email activity, you can better optimize your future sends. Monitoring all of your marketing channels gives you the opportunity to make improvements or eliminate programs that are not resulting in ROI.

Take a look back.

Review your yearly email campaign reports now, to determine how effective your past efforts were. What worked? What didn't? What subject lines got the most open rates? Determine how to develop a high open rate subject line, tailored to your audience based on what you know about them. What types of content received the most clicks? By reviewing these metrics, you will be able to clearly identify a strategy and set goals for next year, without being behind.

Plan ahead.

Having a good content plan is a must for any and all types of marketing. Having a detailed email content and automation plan in place will help you not only be consistent with your communications but you'll have less work to do along the line. Tie your content in with national holidays and industry events. Most importantly, if you send to a large list or a small list it is paramount to keep up-to-date on spam phrases that send your email into the spam folder. Be ahead of the game with spam filters.

Give your email a makeover.

If you've been using the same email template for years, there's no time like the present to give your email marketing a bit of a makeover. If you are a B-to-B company, know that recipients want to skim! Therefore, don't overcrowd your email with unnecessary content that won't be given a second look anyway. It could be as simple as updating your font; or designing a completely new template from scratch. You can match your email colors and appearance to be similar to your website and definitely include beautiful, high-quality and low-resolution photos. Having them be low resolution will help with your mobile optimization and load time. There's nothing worse than having your lead pull up your email but not being able to see the picture you put in there. Email on Acid is a great place to see how your email will look on all different devices and platforms. Your subscribers will appreciate the brand-new look.

Segment.

Segmentation is the key to increasing email marketing metrics and conversion rates for marketing campaigns—and to boosting prospect engagement. With email volumes on the rise and the serious potential for emails to be lost or buried, you can improve your marketing effectiveness by targeting your campaigns to appropriate segments, rather than blasting the same campaign out to all your prospects. Having an unhygienic list and receiving too many soft bounces and hard bounces will also hurt your email deliverability, lowering your sending reputation. Once you have a bad sending reputation, it's easy to get blacklisted, so stay on top of your list and clean regularly!

Optimize for mobile.

If your email design is not optimized to display properly on mobile devices, you risk alienating a huge chunk of your audience. More than half of emails are opened on mobile devices—smartphones and tablets, which will only increasingly dominate.

References and Resources

Interviews

Asher Amiel. Email interview. October 16, 2017

Michael Ballard. Email interview. September 14, 2017

Brad Gurley. Email interview. September 14, 2017

Publications

Campaign Monitor. "Using Emoji and Symbols in Your Email Subject Lines." 2017 https://www.campaignmonitor.com/resources/guides/using-emojis-and-symbols-in-email-marketing/

Courvoisier, Kim. "70 Email Marketing Stats Every Marketer Should Know." *Campaign Monitor.* January 6, 2016

Crowe, Chad. "Google's New Ad Rotation Settings and What They Mean." *Media Shift.* September 29, 2017

http://mediashift.org/2017/09/googles-new-ad-rotation-settings-mean/ Experian Marketing Services. "The Welcome Email Report." October 2010 https://www.experian.com/assets/cheetahmail/whitepapers/welcome-email-report.pdf

Griffis, Alex. "The Truth About Email Panel Data." *250ok.* April 13, 2017 https://250ok.com/email-deliverability/truth-about-email-panel-data/

Grimshaw, John. "DigitalMarketer's 101 Best Email Subject Lines of 2016." *DigitalMarketer.* https://www.digitalmarketer.com/101-best-email-subject-lines-2014/

Jordan, Justine. "How to Write the Perfect Subject Line." Litmus Blog. December 5, 2012. https://litmus.com/blog/how-to-write-the-perfect-subject-line-infographic

Loizos, Connie. "As Uber's Value Slips on the Secondary Market, Lyft's is Rising." *Tech Crunch.* June 22, 2017 https://techcrunch.com/2017/06/22/as-ubers-value-slips-on-the-secondary-market-lyfts-is-rising/

MailChimp Blog. "Subject Line Data: Choose Your Words Wisely." November 13, 2013 https://blog.mailchimp.com/subject-line-data-choose-your-words-wisely/

Marshall, Carla. "By 2019, 80% of the World's Internet Traffic Will be Video (Cisco Case Study)." *Tubular Insights.* June 11, 2015 http://tubularinsights.com/2019-internet-video-traffic/

Nanji, Ayaz. "The Five Most Effective (and Ineffective) Words in Email Subject lines." *MarketingProfs.* February 9, 2015 http://www.marketingprofs.com/charts/2015/26984/five-most-effective-and-ineffective-words-in-email-subject-lines

Patel, Kunur. "Groupon Marketing Spending Works Almost Too Well." *Ad Age.* November 2, 2011 http://adage.com/article/digital/groupon-marketing-spending-works/230777/

van Rijn, Jordie. "The Ultimate Mobile Email Statistics Overview." *emailmonday.* https://www.emailmonday.com/mobile-email-usage-statistics

Postmaster Tools and Reputation Sites

AnubisNetworks Mailspike, http://mailspike.org

AOL, https://www.aol.com

App River, https://www.appriver.com

Apple Mail, https://support.apple.com/mail

AudiencePoint, http://audiencepoint.com

Barracuda, https://www.barracuda.com

BlueTie, https://bluetie.com/en/

CAN-SPAM Rule, https://www.ftc.gov/enforcement/rules/rulemaking-regulatory-reform-proceedings/can-spam-rule

Canada's Anti-Spam Legislation, http://fightspam.gc.ca/eic/site/030.nsf/eng/home

Cisco Systems, Inc. SpamCop, https://www.spamcop.net

Cloudmark Sender Intelligence, https://www.cloudmark.com/en/s/products/cloudmark-sender-intelligence

Comcast Xfinity, https://www.xfinity.com

Cox Communications, https://www.cox.com/residential/home.html

Cyren Email Security, https://www.cyren.com/products/email-security-gateway

DomainKeys Identified Mail, http://www.dkim.org

Domain Message Authentication Reporting and Conformance, https://dmarc.org

EarthLink, http://www.earthlink.net

Email on Acid, https://www.emailonacid.com

EU General Data Protection Regulation, http://www.eugdpr.org

FastMail, https://www.fastmail.com

Get Response, https://www.getresponse.com/?marketing_gv=np

Gmail, https://www.google.com/gmail/about/

Hubspot, https://www.hubspot.com

IBM X-Force, https://www.ibm.com/security/xforce/

Inbox Pros, https://inboxpros.com/

Korea Internet and Security Agency, http://www.kisa.or.kr/eng/main.jsp

Mailgun, https://www.mailgun.com

McAfee Trusted Source, https://www.trustedsource.org

Network Solutions, https://www.networksolutions.com

Office 365, https://products.office.com/en-US/?ms.url=office365com

Oracle Marketing Cloud, https://www.oracle.com/marketingcloud/index.html

Outlook.com Smart Network Data Services, https://postmaster.live.com/snds/

Proofpoint, https://www.proofpoint.com/us

Rackspace, https://www.rackspace.com/en-us

Register.com, https://www.register.com

Return Path Sender Score, https://www.senderscore.org

Salesforce.com, https://www.salesforce.com

Sender Policy Framework, http://www.openspf.org

SmartScreen Filter, https://support.microsoft.com/en-us/help/17443/windows-internet-explorer-smartscreen-filter-faq

SonicWall, https://www.sonicwall.com/en-us/home

Sophos, https://www.sophos.com/en-us.aspx

Spam and Open Relay Blocking System, http://www.sorbs.net

Spamhaus, https://www.spamhaus.org/

SURBL, http://www.surbl.org

Symantec Brightmail, https://www.symantec.com

Synacor, https://synacor.com

Talos, https://www.talosintelligence.com/reputation_center

Telenor Group, https://www.telenor.com

Thunderbird, https://www.mozilla.org/en-US/thunderbird/

Trend Micro, https://www.trendmicro.com/en_us/business.html

Trustwave, https://www.trustwave.com/Home/

United Online, http://www.untd.com/company/overview/

WatchGuard ReputationAuthority, http://reputationauthority.org/index.php

Web of Trust, https://www.mywot.com

Web.com Group, https://www1.web.com

Webroot, https://www.webroot.com/us/en

Yahoo!, https://www.Yahoo.com

Yandex, https://yandex.com

Zoho, https://www.zoho.com

Key Terms of Deliverability—Grasp and Mastery for Paradise

Blacklist

A list of IP addresses and/or domains that are not allowed access into a particular network. By being blacklisted, the sender's emails may bounce and/or get rejected.

DKIM (Domain Keys Identified Mail)

The most comprehensive email authentication standard that signs each outgoing message with an encrypted key. While SPF involves making changing to DNS records, DKIM requires senders to change the way that messages are constructed.

Email client

Software that downloads email from your provider, or that an individual uses to access their email online. An example would be Microsoft Outlook.

Email Authentication

IP and domain authentication is your "passport" to the Inbox. Essentially, this authentication verifies that you are allowed to send using the sending IP address and the sending domain. Authentication helps to prevent phishing and spoofing of your domain, as well as lets your recipients know that you have taken the precautions of using IP and domain authentication.

Feedback loop

When the mailbox provider forwards complaints of recipients to the organization that sent the email. Typically, this is sent back to the Email Service Provider that sent the email. Not all mailbox providers and networks maintain a feedback loop, but it is important to get signed up with all that are available. If you use an Email Service Provider, they will typically take care of this.

Hard bounce

This bounce rejection reason from the recipient mail server indicates a permanent delivery failure. Retried delivery attempts will not be successful. An example of a hard bounce would be a bad mailbox.

IP Address

A number assigned to each computer, network device, or network in order to distinguish each network interface and networked device. Marketers also use an IP address to send out email campaigns. The IP may or may not be dedicated to a particular sender/marketer.

ISP (Internet Service Provider)

Provides access to the Internet and normally provides the user an email address associated with that provider. An example ISP would be Comcast.

MBP (Mailbox Provider)

Provides email hosting and storage. It implements email servers to send, receive, accept, and store email for end users. An example MBP would be Gmail.

Soft bounce

This bounce rejection reason from the recipient mail server indicates a transient delivery failure. Retried delivery attempts may be successful. An example of a soft bounce would be mailbox full.

SPF (Sender Policy Framework)

An email authentication standard that specifies what IP addresses can send mail for a given domain. This is the easiest authentication standard to implement and is most widely used, but does not account for the visible headers in the message, such as the from and reply-to address.

Whitelist

A list of IP addresses and/or domains that are allowed into a particular network. By being whitelisted, the sender also bypasses typical "checks" designed to quarantine emails.

Deliverability Monitoring Terms

AOL

A B-to-C mailbox provider that blocks on erratic volume, abuse complaints, bounces, and spam trap hits. AOL scans each IP that delivers mail and assigns it a reputation of Neutral, Good, Bad or Undisclosed.

Barracuda

Barracuda Reputation System is a real-time database of IP addresses that have a 'poor' reputation for sending valid emails. Barracuda Central maintains and manually verifies all IP addresses marked as 'poor' on the Barracuda Reputation System. By combining both the IP and reputation data, Barracuda Networks can easily determine whether a message is spam or legitimate email. In addition to IP reputation, the Barracuda Central team maintains reputation on URLs, which gives the Barracuda Spam and Virus Firewall the ability to quickly block an email based on a poorly-rated URL contained in the message. Once identified, Barracuda Central can implement countermeasures to mitigate these threats.

Cloudmark

Cloudmark Sender Intelligence (CSI) is a comprehensive sender monitoring and analysis system that delivers timely and accurate reputation and categorization for different senders. CSI combines real-time data from Cloudmark's Global Threat Network system. The Global Threat Network monitors traffic from all Cloudmark Authority installations worldwide, representing over 15% of all internet email traffic.

Comcast

An Internet Service Provider that provides email addresses for their subscribers. Comcast will block on bad email addresses, spam traps, and user complaints. Comcast will also rate limit the amount of emails into their network based upon IP reputation.

CYREN

A leading provider of cloud-based security solutions that deliver powerful protection. CYREN's GlobalView Cloud is fueled by patented Recurrent Pattern Detection technology to deliver Web Security, Email Security, and AntiMalware solutions with uncompromising protection in both embedded and security-as-a-service deployment models.

EarthLink

A B-to-C mailbox provider and ISP, but is focusing more and more on B-to-B hosting and email. EarthLink blocks on spam trap hits, complaints, and erratic volume within their network.

Gmail

A webmail email provider that has aggressive filtering technology based upon recipient engagement. Gmail includes a tabbed Inbox setting, but will also now download images by default. Gmail does not offer a typical feedback loop and we highly recommend segmenting out those recipients with low engagement metrics.

Mailspike

A service intended to provide all receivers and reputation providers a baseline of data to help block the senders with the worst reputations. The reputation data is compiled on top of specific characteristics and over-time behavior of IP addresses seen sending email. The reputation data compiles a score, which will dictate the likelihood of an IP address being used to send spam.

Microsoft Smart Network Data Services (SNDS)

A revolutionary Windows Live Hotmail initiative designed to allow everyone who owns IP space to contribute to the fight against spam, malware, viruses, and other Internet evils, to protect e-mail and the Internet as a valued communications, productivity and commerce tool. By providing that data to service providers, most of whom wouldn't otherwise have access to any such data, they are empowered to use their relationship with their customers to react and take repair actions, such as preventing spam from originating within their IP space. The overarching goal of SNDS is to make the Internet a better, safer place. Working together, Windows Live Hotmail and service providers can make their respective customers happier and more satisfied with the various services we all provide.

Network Solutions

Provides services such as web hosting, website design, email, and online marketing. Sometimes, legitimate email is blocked or "blacklisted" when large amounts of spam are detected from an IP address.

Office 365

The brand name used by Microsoft for subscription-based productivity software and related services. There are multiple layers of filtering within Office 365 including connection, authentication, reputation, content, and blacklist. We are able to pinpoint and remove Office 365 blocks as they occur.

Register.com

Provide a range of resources usually reserved for larger organizations, from Web hosting, Web site design, e-commerce, search engine marketing, SSL Certificates, email and domain name registration services, including WHOIS services. Sometimes, legitimate email is blocked or "blacklisted" when large amounts of spam are detected from an IP address.

ReputationAuthority

This service incorporates data from multiple sources including discovered threats from all WatchGuard XCS customers, proprietary global email and Web reputation databases, and third-party systems from across the globe. The combination of these feeds are automatically updated in the WatchGuard reputation database and streamed instantly across the ReputationAuthority network in real-time, providing organizations with a completely automated system for rejecting email and web threats. The scores, including clean and spam, are only measuring the emails going through the WatchGuard platform.

Talos

Provides a view into real-time threat intelligence across web and email. Talos is powered by Cisco Security Intelligence Operations (SIO), a cloud-based capability of daily security intelligence across over 1.6 million deployed Web, Email, Firewall and IPS appliances. SIO's intelligence is augmented by a network of traps, crawlers, third-party partnerships and threat research.

Sender Score

Like a bank running your credit score to gauge your credit history but measures the health of your email program. Sender Score is a number between 0 and 100 that identifies your sender reputation and shows you how mailbox providers view your IP address. Scores above 80 are good, but closer to 100 are best! Mailbox providers take a lot of metrics into consideration to determine your sender reputation including spam complaints, mailing to unknown users, industry blacklists, and more.

SonicWALL

Comprehensive Anti-Spam Service (CASS) offers small-to-medium-sized businesses comprehensive protection from spam and viruses, with instant deployment over existing SonicWALL firewalls. CASS offers complete inbound anti-spam, anti-phishing, anti-malware protection and features, SonicWALL Global Response Intelligent Defense (GRID) Network IP Reputation, Advanced Content Management, Denial of Service prevention, full quarantine and customizable per-user junk summaries. CASS offers >98% effectiveness against spam, dropping >80% of spam at the gateway, while utilizing advanced anti-spam techniques like Adversarial Variational Bayes filtering on remaining email.

Sophos

Monitors spam and web threats as they happen and are collected in a dashboard in real time. Sophos maintains IP address classifications that can be used by receiving networks to reject, not deliver, or quarantine spam messages in Sophos anti-spam products.

Symantec

Uses various methods and data sources to create lists of IP addresses that are suspected of being untrustworthy. Listings are mostly due to complaints and spam trap hits. These are given ratings of blocked or not blocked.

Trend Micro

A global network operated by highly trained spam investigators who research, collect, process, and distribute reputation ratings of good or bad on IP addresses. These specialists monitor spam activity, develop information on spam sources and verify the accuracy of reputation ratings.

TrustedSource

Works by analyzing in real-time traffic patterns from email, web and network data flows from McAfee's global set of security appliances and hosted services. Working off that data stream, it applies data mining and analysis techniques to determine the degree of maliciousness and security risk associated with each Internet identity, as well as perform content categorization.

Trustwave

Email IP Reputation Service is a database of IP addresses compiled by Trustwave. These IP addresses have been reported as sources of Unsolicited Bulk Email. Trustwave does not recommend acceptance of email originating from these IP addresses. Trustwave makes this reputation listing available to Trustwave customers for use in scanning email. The choice to use the listing, and the action taken on any IP address that is listed, are at the sole discretion of the customer.

Web.com Group, Inc.

A provider of Web services and email catering to small- and medium-sized businesses. Sometimes, legitimate email is blocked or "blacklisted" when large amounts of spam are detected from an IP address.

Webroot

A cloud-based, real-time internet threat detection for consumers, businesses and enterprises. Webroot delivers real-time advanced internet threat protection to customers through its BrightCloud security intelligence platform and its SecureAnywhere suite of security products for endpoints, mobile devices and corporate networks.

Yahoo!

A webmail email provider that also provides email filtering and hosting for other email providers. Yahoo! relies heavily on recipient engagement, complaints, and content. Yahoo! offers a feedback loop and a Postmaster page with best practices.

About the Author

Chris Arrendale has more than 16 years of experience in the technology and software industry and has worked directly with many different ISPs, mailbox providers, spam filter providers, blacklists, and partners to resolve email deliverability and privacy issues. Chris graduated with his AA from Oxford College of Emory University, BA from Emory University and his MS from Southern Polytechnic State University.

He also maintains several professional certifications including Certified Information Privacy Professional (CIPM, CIPT, CIPP/US, CIPP/G, FIP), Certificate of Cloud Security Knowledge (CCSK), as well as many marketing automation and email service provider certifications. Chris is actively involved with the Email Experience Council (EEC), Messaging, Malware and Mobile Anti-Abuse Working Group (M3AAWG), Email Sender and Provider Coalition (ESPC), International Association of Privacy Professionals (IAPP), and the Atlanta Interactive Marketing Association (AIMA). Since founding Inbox Pros, an email deliverability and privacy consulting firm, Chris has worked with a variety of clients across many verticals solving their deliverability and compliance challenges.

Deliverability Inferno is Chris's debut as an author.

CPSIA information can be obtained
at www.ICGtesting.com
Printed in the USA
BVOW09s0747160418
513497BV00008B/54/P